Moreton Morre

(022)

Marketing

SAGE COURSE COMPANIONS
KNOWLEDGE AND SKILLS *for* SUCCESS

Marketing
Jim Blythe

SAGE Publications
London ● Thousand Oaks ● New Delhi

SAGE Publications Ltd
1 Oliver's Yard
55 City Road
London EC1Y 1SP

SAGE Publications Inc.
2455 Teller Road
Thousand Oaks, California 91320

SAGE Publications India Pvt Ltd
B-42, Panchsheel Enclave
Post Box 4109
New Delhi 110 017

British Library Cataloguing in Publication data

A catalogue record for this book is available from
the British Library

ISBN-10 1-4129-1033-1   ISBN-13 978-1-4129-1033-0
ISBN-10 1-4129-1034-X   ISBN-13 978-1-4129-1034-7 (pbk)

Library of Congress Control Number: 2005904554

Typeset by C&M Digitals (P) Ltd., Chennai, India
Printed in Great Britain by The Cromwell Press Ltd, Trowbridge, Wiltshire
Printed on paper from sustainable resources

contents

part one

introducing your companion	

This SAGE Course Companion offers you an insider's guide into how to make the most of your undergraduate course, and extend your understanding of key concepts covered in the course. It will provide essential help with revising for your course exams, preparing and writing course assessment materials, and enhancing and progressing your knowledge and thinking skills in line with course requirements.

This book should be used as a supplement to your textbook and lecture notes. You may want to glance through it quickly, reading it in parallel with your course syllabus, and note where each topic is covered in both the syllabus and this Companion. Ideally, you should buy this book at the beginning of your course – it will provide you with a quick explanation of any topics you are having trouble with, and of course the advice on getting the most from your course will not be much help if you have already finished!

It isn't intended to replace your textbooks or lectures – it is intended to save you time when you are revising for your exams or preparing coursework. Note that *re*-vision implies that you looked at the subject the first time round!

The Companion will help you to anticipate exam questions and gives guidelines on what your examiners will be looking for. It should be seen as a framework in which to organise the subject matter, and to extract the most important points from your textbooks, lecture notes, and other learning materials on your course.

This book should direct you to the key issues (and key thinkers) in the marketing field. Whichever textbook you are using, the basics are the basics: we have given some guidance on where topics are covered in specific books, but you should read the Companion in parallel with your textbook and identify where subjects are covered in more detail in both your text and in your course syllabus.

There is also a study and revision skills guide in Part 3 which will help you to learn more efficiently. Learning is best accomplished by seeing the information from several different angles – which is why you attend lectures and tutorials, read the textbook, and read around the subject in general. This book will help you to bring together these different sources.

How to use this book

Ideally, you should have already bought this book before your course starts, so that you can get a quick overview of each topic before you go into the lecture – but if you didn't do this, all is not lost. The Companion will still be equally helpful as a revision guide, and as a way of directing you to the key thinkers and writers on marketing.

The first section is about how to think like a marketer: it will help you to get into the mindset of the subject and think about it critically. As a bonus, of course, it also means learning how to think like your examiner! Examiners want to see that you can handle the basic concepts of the subject: if you need a quick overview of the background to marketing, this is the section you will find most useful.

The next section goes into the curriculum in more detail, taking each topic and providing you with the key elements. Again, this does not substitute for the deeper coverage you will have had in your lectures and texts, but it does provide a quick revision guide, or a 'primer' to use before lectures.

You can use this book either to give yourself a head start before you start studying marketing, in other words give yourself a preview course, or it can be used as a revision aid, or of course both. Each section contains within it the following features:

- Tips on handling the information in exams, or reminders of key issues: this will help you to anticipate exam questions, and help you remember the main points to bring in when answering them.

- Examples: these are useful for putting the theory into a 'real-world' context, and can of course be used in exams to illustrate the points you make.
- Running themes: the areas that will always be of interest to a marketer. You will find that these can almost always be brought into an exam question, and you will be expected to do so. Running themes are highlighted in bold throughout the book.
- Input from key thinkers in the field: these will be useful to quote in exams, as well as providing you with the main influences in the development of marketing.
- Sample exam questions with outline answers: these should help you be better prepared for the actual questions, even though they will (of course) be different.
- Ideas for answering assignment questions: these should give you some ideas for the structure and content of essays based on the topics covered here.
- Taking it Further section: this is about taking your thinking a stage beyond simply laying out the current 'received wisdom'. The Taking it Further section introduces some criticality, often from 'sharp end' academic thinking, and will help you to take a broader conceptual view of the topic: on a practical level, this is the type of thinking that moves you from a pass to a first!

Part 3 of this Companion is a study guide which will help you with getting more from your lectures, remembering more when you are sitting exams, and with writing essays.

A glossary of key terms is included at the back of the book. Key terms have been highlighted in a different font so that they are easy to spot, for example **deontology**.

Thinking like a marketer

Marketing is a relatively young discipline, and it is important to note that there is still considerable disagreement and debate among academics and practitioners about what marketing is and is not. In particular, there is disagreement about what the boundaries of marketing are.

The key principle agreed on by all marketing academics is that marketing places the customer at the centre of all marketing thought. This does not mean that marketing is a charitable institution: organisations exist to fulfil their own aims, but marketers argue that all organisational activities should be informed and driven by **customers** and **consumers**. In practice, following this principle is not always easy: customers are not necessarily consumers (consider a mother buying clothes for a small child) and customers may have different needs from consumers. Also, it is extremely easy to make assumptions about what consumers **need** and want – often these prejudices are based on what the planner needs and wants, not on what the actual consumers need and want. The end product of marketing is the competitive advantage of the firm: firms which look after their customers should do better than firms which do not. In simple terms, marketers put customers at the centre of everything they do because it is the best way to get their money off them.

> *If you take only one thing away from your marketing course, take this: in any question in marketing, always start with the customer!*

Marketing practice can be considered as being all the activities that happen at the interface between the company and the outside world. Different writers have different views on how broad this interface should be: some believe that it should be limited to customers only, others believe that marketing has a role in all contact with outsiders, and even with employees and other 'insiders'.

Another popular way of considering marketing's role is to define it as managing exchange. Marketing is a process of developing products and services so that they provide benefits for consumers, then offering them in exchange for money. The terms, place, time and conditions for the exchange are managed by the marketer. This definition does have some conceptual difficulties, because consumers often have a role in deciding many of these issues (particularly dealing on the Internet – consider e-Bay). However, in recent years it has become a useful way of defining the borders of marketing.

As an academic discipline, marketing has developed from a number of other disciplines. The first of these is economics, from which marketing took the concepts of supply and demand, of the **economic choice**, and of **price elasticity of demand**. From sociology, marketing took concepts of self-image, of peer group pressure, and concepts of the family. From psychology, marketers took perception theory, learning, and decision-making theory. From anthropology, marketers have derived theories of culture and its effect on international marketing.

Marketing thought is often supposed to have gone through a series of conceptual changes, as follows:

1 **The production era:** the theory is that at one time the key to competitive success was to produce as much as possible of a limited range of products at the lowest possible price. At the beginning of the

mass-production era, in the nineteenth and early twentieth centuries, this was probably true. Factory-produced goods were so much cheaper than hand-made tailored goods that companies came to believe that making goods even cheaper would lead to even greater success.

2 **The product era:** companies found that producing a standard product for a low price was not sufficient. Consumers were becoming more demanding, and wanted to move away from the standardised products on offer and buy something with more features. Companies therefore began to add extra features to their products, but since different consumers have different needs the list of features grew ever-longer and consequently the cost of the products grew.

3 **The sales era:** mass production meant that too many goods were following too few customers. At this point, firms decided that the key to success was to have a powerful and aggressive sales effort, using high-pressure techniques to persuade people to buy. Sales orientation assumes that customers will buy more than they need if they are pressured, that clever sales techniques will persuade people, that people will not object to this process and will be prepared to buy again in future, and that people's misgivings about buying represent sales resistance rather than anything inherently wrong with the product. Theodore Levitt famously said that 'selling is about the needs of the seller; marketing is about the needs of the buyer' (Levitt, 1960).

4 **The marketing era:** at this point, companies realised that goods had to meet customer needs, and that it is actually easier to change the company and its products than it is to change the customers. Putting customer needs at the centre of the firm's activities became the key concept in marketing.

5 **Societal marketing era:** the concept of societal marketing was first proposed in the 1970s. Essentially, societal marketing is about meeting customer needs within the context of meeting the needs of society as a whole. It has achieved a greater prominence in the 1990s and early twenty-first century because it allows for the concept of sustainability and even environmentalism.

This history of the development of marketing thought actually has little relationship to the history of commerce, but it does offer a logical structure and is frequently quoted, especially in American textbooks. Societal marketing is credited to Philip Kotler, often regarded as the father of modern marketing. Kotler tends towards the view that everything in life has a connection to marketing and can be considered through a marketing lens: not everyone subscribes to this view, particularly in Europe. Note that Kotler's view is closer to the 'marketing as interface between the organisation and the outside' view than to the 'managing exchange' view.

The related terminology for this view of the development of marketing thought is as follows:

- Production orientation, production philosophy, production concept.
- Product orientation, product philosophy.
- Sales orientation, selling orientation, selling concept.
- Marketing orientation, consumer orientation, marketing concept.
- Societal orientation, societal marketing concept.

Any of the above terms might appear in different texts, or be used by different writers and lecturers.

Each of these orientations is about making the firm more competitive. Marketing orientation and even societal orientation are ultimately about the success of the firm – don't start imagining that it is about developing a social conscience!

Marketing subdivides into a number of specialist disciplines, although there is considerable overlap between them. These disciplines are:

- Consumer behaviour: this is behavioural science (psychology, sociology, anthropology) applied to people's economic behaviour. Understandably, this is a large topic area, since consumers are at the centre of marketing. It is often taught as 'buyer behaviour' in order to include industrial buyer behaviour.
- Marketing communications: this covers all forms of communications which are intended to facilitate or propose an exchange. Note the word 'facilitate' – some marketing communication (notably corporate advertising and public relations) does not directly seek to offer a product, but is aimed at improving the corporate reputation so that people are more likely to buy the products in future. Because marketing communications travel via many different routes, the subject is itself subdivided into advertising, public relations, sales management, and sales promotion: more recently, electronic marketing (e-commerce) has emerged as a sub-discipline.
- Marketing strategy: this is sometimes also called strategic marketing. Strategy is about creating competitive advantage, so it is concerned with positioning the company and its products effectively relative to competitors. The first decision to be made is what business the company is in – as defined by customers. For example, a hairdressing firm might define itself as a hairdressing salon, which is a definition derived from the firm's perspective: from

the customer's perspective, a hairdressing salon is in the business of raising people's morale and self-esteem. Marketing strategy can refer to those activities directly concerned with marketing (i.e. operating within the overall corporate strategy), whereas strategic marketing is sometimes used to refer to using marketing to create a corporate strategy. Having said that, the terms are often used interchangeably.

- New product development: developing products so that they meet consumer needs better is a marketing role, although obviously engineers and designers have a strong role.
- Services marketing: there is some debate among marketing academics as to whether services are conceptually different from physical products in terms of how they should be marketed: they reason that most services contain an element of physical product, and vice versa. However, the marketing of services remains a separate topic area, with texts and even journals devoted to it.
- International marketing: marketing becomes more complex when products and promotions cross national and cultural boundaries.
- Business-to-business marketing: B2B marketing is a relatively new addition to marketing thinking: most marketing courses predominantly teach business-to-consumer marketing (B2C). For an introductory course, this enables students to relate to the subject better, but in fact B2B markets do exhibit different characteristics from B2C markets, and are also considerably larger.
- Not-for-profit marketing: some organisations such as charities and government departments use marketing techniques to persuade or inform their contributors or 'customers'. Because these organisations do not measure their success in terms of profit (although charities, at least, do aim to generate surpluses) the study of the special techniques involved is called not-for-profit marketing.

Marketers operate by controlling various elements of the marketing mix. The marketing mix is all the activities undertaken by marketers, and was first defined by McCarthy in the early 1960s as comprising four elements (the four Ps). These are:

1 *Product:* the bundle of benefits offered by the organisation.

2 *Price:* the consideration given by the customer for the product.

3 *Promotion:* the communications about the product which are aimed at the consumers.

4 *Place:* the location where the exchange takes place.

Although the 4P model is widely taught, and is often the basis on which textbooks are structured, it suffers from a number of flaws. First, it is incomplete – there are many other activities that marketers carry out which are not part of the model. Second, it tends to put each activity into a separate category, whereas in fact they overlap considerably. This is a criticism which has been associated with Shelby Hunt in particular. Third, it tends to imply that marketing is something which is done to people, rather than something that implies mutual benefit between marketer and consumer.

> *Remember that all the elements of the mix affect all the other elements: separating the elements is only a way of breaking down the problem.*

An addition to the model was made by Booms and Bitner in 1981, in order to recognise the different nature of services marketing. Booms and Bitner proposed adding three more Ps: people, process and physical evidence. Further attempts to add more Ps have been made, but most marketing courses operate with either a 4P or a 7P model.

Almost all marketing courses and marketing textbooks begin by seeking to define marketing. This is because marketing is frequently thought (by non-marketers) to be solely about advertising or selling. This is an easy mistake to make, because advertising and selling are the most obvious aspects of marketing. However, like an iceberg, nine-tenths of marketing is invisible to the general public.

Virtually all marketing courses and textbooks begin by seeking to define what marketing is (some also define what it is not). Marketing has been defined in many different ways by different authors and organisations. The two most commonly-quoted definitions come from the UK's Chartered Institute of Marketing, and from the American Marketing Association. Here are the main definitions:

- Chartered Institute of Marketing (www.cim.co.uk): 'Marketing is the management process which identifies, anticipates, and supplies customer requirements efficiently and profitably'.
- American Marketing Association (www.marketingpower.com): 'Marketing is the process of planning and executing the conception, pricing, promotion and distribution of ideas, goods and services to create exchange and satisfy individual and organisational objectives'.
- Philip Kotler (1997): 'Marketing is a social and managerial process by which individuals and groups obtain what they need and want through creating and exchanging products and value with others'.
- Adcock, Halborg and Ross (2001): 'Marketing is the study of exchange processes especially those associated with the provision of goods and services'.

Each of these definitions can be criticised in some ways. The CIM definition does not take account of not-for-profit marketing, and does not mention informing consumers, or indeed anything else to do with promotion, which is after all an important part of marketing. The AMA definition is better, since it talks about organisational and personal objectives rather than profit, but it still implies that marketing is something which is done to people in a paternalistic way. Kotler's definition has been criticised because it is simply too broad – if marketing covers all kinds of exchanges, then is a mother's promise to take a child to the zoo if he tidies his room also part of marketing? Most people would say not. The same criticism applies to the Adcock et al. definition.

You may well be asked to compare and contrast the different definitions of marketing. None of these definitions are perfect – you are allowed to criticise them!

Taking it **FURTHER**

You may be asked to critique theory, and even if you are not it is no bad thing to do so anyway. At undergraduate level, you are not really required to show criticality, but at Masters level you will be expected to do so in order to produce work of Masters quality.

Criticality means that you have thought about the theories you are being presented with, not merely remembered them. If you disagree with a theory, and can argue the case well enough, it will be to your credit – as long as you really understood the theory in the first place! Throughout this guide there will be points at which the theory will be critiqued: obviously you will form your own ideas, and you should not be afraid to use them, but the Taking it Further boxes are intended to show you how to critique theory.

A quick note on studying at Masters level is indicated here: note that most of the academics who teach you (and most of those who developed the theories you are studying) are probably only qualified to Masters level themselves (though some will have PhDs). When we give you a Masters degree, we are in effect saying that you are at the same level as us – so we expect you to join in the debate as an equal. That is why demonstrating criticality is essential at Masters level.

part two

core areas of the curriculum	

Running themes in marketing

There are certain themes which will always be relevant to almost any question in marketing. We will return to these throughout the book, but you need to keep these in mind when answering questions in exams or assignments. They are as follows:

1 *Customer centrality*: this is far and away the most important theme, but equally it is the hardest to practise!

2 *Meeting organisational objectives*: through helping customers to reach their objectives.

3 *Managing exchange*: this means promoting exchanges as well as handling the actual processes.

4 *Customer perception of brands and organisations.*

5 *Market segmentation*: dividing the market into groups of people with similar needs is crucial to effective marketing.

Obviously curricula differ somewhat between different teaching institutions. You may therefore find that the order of subjects also differs somewhat from your course, but you should be able to find all the topics here somewhere!

Most marketing lecturers (like most academics of any discipline) have favourite topics and subjects, and also have pet hates. You should try to work out what these are, because it will give you some guidance in what to expect in the exam, and what NOT to write!

Each section below gives a quick overview of the key issues in the topic, and a sample exam question, with an outline of the issues you should cover in the answer. In all cases, you should keep in mind the running themes described above: referring to the wider issues will almost always gain you marks, provided of course you do not wander away from the question too much!

| 1 | |
| the underpinnings of marketing | |

Marketing emerged as an academic discipline from a combination of behavioural sciences and economics. It is largely a practical subject however: in many ways marketing lacks the necessary boundaries and rigour to be a purely academic subject.

Economic theory has contributed the following main concepts (these are from the **managing exchange** running theme):

1 *The theory of supply and demand:* the assumption is that for most goods, prices will rise as supply shrinks, but demand also shrinks as prices rise. If supply increases, prices will drop and demand will rise, so supply and demand should always balance out. In practice this theory is too simplistic – for some goods, demand will fall as price falls and vice versa.

2 *Economic choice:* The assumption is that if one spends money on one item, one is therefore choosing not to buy a different item. This theory underpins marketing theories of competition – that firms do not only compete with other firms which produce similar items, they also compete with firms which fulfil a similar need for the consumer.

This is a typical example of the need to think like a consumer. Cinemas are in competition with other forms of entertainment, not just with other cinemas, which means they also compete with pubs, restaurants, libraries, etc.

3 **Price elasticity of demand:** For some goods, the fall-off in demand as prices rise is minimal (for example, table salt). For other products, demand drops dramatically if there is even a small price increase (for example, borrowed money). Knowing how elastic the price is helps determine the prices the firm should charge for the product, and also marketers are often able to affect the elasticity of demand for their products by (for example) improving customer loyalty or making their brand the most desirable on the market.

4 **Indifference curves/Edgeworth box: Indifference curves** predict that people are prepared to substitute one product for another, up to a point. People are said to be indifferent as to whether they have X quantity of one product, and Y of another, or vice-versa. The Edgeworth Box predicts that trade between people with different indifference curves will result in both individuals being better off as a result.

Remember that trade always results in both parties being better off. Value is not absolute: it is only relevant to the individual, so a trade will only happen when one individual thinks that a product is worth more than it is to the other individual. If this were not so, trade would be impossible.

5 **Competition theory: Monopolies** are situations where one firm controls the market; **oligopoly** is a situation in which several firms control the market between them, often via agreements (either these agreements are made in secret, which is illegal, or there is an 'understanding' between the firms that none of them will start a price war). **Perfect competition** is a situation in which customers and suppliers have full knowledge of the markets, and prices are set by supply and demand processes alone. Such markets are extremely rare: only the international money markets and stock exchanges fit the description. The commonest form of competition is **monopolistic competition,** in which one firm dominates the market without really controlling it completely, so that other firms are free to enter.

Economics tends to assume that people are more rational than is in fact the case. Marketers therefore draw on behavioural science disciplines to explain the irrational (or emotional) aspects of people's purchasing behaviour.

Sociology is the study of group behaviour. It has contributed the following concepts to marketing:

1 *Self-image:* people often make purchases because they want to impress other people, or because the purchase fits in with an image they are trying to develop.

2 *Reference groups:* People refer to other people in order to know what to do in a given situation. Groups might be **aspirational** (groups we want to belong to) or **dissociative** (we would prefer other people not to think we are in these groups). **Primary groups** are those which we see every day (family and friends); **secondary groups** are those we see occasionally for specific purposes (e.g. clubs, professional associations). Groups might be **formal** (with a known, fixed membership such as sports club) or **informal** (membership just happens, as with groups of friends).

> *Family is probably the most important reference group. However, in recent years families have become fragmented – the mother, father and two children model of family accounts for less than 10 per cent of UK households.*

3 *Geodemographics:* where people live, what they do for a living, how well-educated they are, how old they are, and their ethnic background all influence consumption behaviour. Geodemographic data is used to divide people into groups (market segments) with similar needs. This theory is therefore about the **segmentation** running theme.

4 *Social class:* where people are positioned relative to other members of society. Many of the old class distinctions have disappeared, only to be replaced by new ones. Classifying people according to a number of criteria including education, income, and job type is the basis of social class: certain behaviours (including consumption behaviours) are expected from members of the same social class.

5 *Normative compliance:* this is the pressure exerted by the group on its members to conform with group ideals of acceptable behaviour. This includes purchasing behaviour – for example, a cricket club

will expect members to buy cricket bats, not tennis rackets, but at a more subtle level will expect members to wear white clothes when playing and to behave themselves in the club house. Singing dirty songs is expected in rugby teams, but not in bridge clubs.

Anthropology is the study of culture, which is a collective set of beliefs, values, knowledge, language and customs held by an identifiable group of people. This again refers to the **segmentation** running theme. Anthropology has contributed the following:

1 *Concepts of culture as a centralising influence:* normative compliance is again used here.

2 *Sub-cultures within the main culture:* a sub-culture is one which agrees with almost all the beliefs of the main culture, but has extra beliefs of its own, or even some disagreement with the main culture. For example, a teenage street gang might develop new words, but still speak English; the same group might behave anarchically, but still believe in democracy (voting on activities, for example).

Psychology is the study of individual thought processes. It has contributed the following to marketing:

1 *Perception theory:* perception is about the way we build up a 'mental map' of how the world works. Perception is both analytic and synthetic: we do not absorb everything that is thrown at us, so the 'mental map' has gaps in it, which we fill by inventing (synthesising) information to make the picture complete. This is why people have differing views of the world. This is about the **customer perception** running theme.

People say 'perception' when they really mean 'untrue'. This is not strictly correct – for the individual, their perception of the world is reality. Perceptions are not necessarily false!

2 *Learning behaviour: classical conditioning* comes about by associating a stimulus with a response, as evidenced by Pavlov's dogs. After a period of repetition, responses become automatic. *Operant conditioning* refers to rewarding (or punishing) behaviour until 'correct' behaviour becomes automatic. Cognitive learning is conscious learning, without direct reinforcement (much as you are doing now). Rote learning is learning by repetition (reading the same words over and

over until you remember them automatically). Vicarious learning means learning from observing others – this is useful for marketers, because they can show appropriate behaviours in advertisements in the hope that consumers will imitate the behaviour.

3 *Reasoning:* this is the process of analysis and thinking which enables us to draw usable conclusions from limited data. Some advertising puts arguments forward, often ending with a question, with the intention of letting people draw their own conclusions. It is commonly used in political advertising.

4 *Personality:* the collective traits, beliefs, values and attitudes which distinguish one individual from another. Personality can be used as a segmentation variable.

> *For a psychologist, personality is not the same as charisma. We all have a personality: it does not equate to anything desirable or undesirable, it is merely a description of factors.*

5 *Attitude:* attitude is composed of **cognition** (what we know) **affect** (what we feel) and **conation** (what we believe). Attitudes can be changed by changing any one of these elements. This is useful for the **segmentation** theme as well as the **customer perception** theme.

6 *Motivation:* this is the force that drives behaviour. It has direction as well as quantity. Three key thinkers have contributed to our knowledge of motivation: Maslow, with his famous hierarchy of need, Herzburg, with his dual-factor theory, and Vroom, who outlined expectancy theory. Motivation is linked to wants and needs: a need is an unfulfilled lack of something, a want is a specific satisfier.

> *Note that, for human beings, needs go far beyond mere survival. People in the Western world have long since moved on from survival needs – these are no longer an issue. Do not fall into the trap of confusing needs with the necessities of life.*

> *You may be asked to compare and contrast these theories, or apply them in some way. They are not in fact mutually exclusive: Herzburg's hygiene factors correspond well with Maslow's survival factors, and Vroom's contribution complements both theories because it includes the individual's expectation that the goal can be achieved and is desirable.*

Taking it **_FURTHER_**

Maslow's hierarchy of need supposedly shows that people will not become interested in higher needs (esteem, self-actuallsation, etc.) until lower needs have been satisfied (physical needs). So how do we explain the artist who goes without meals in order to finish a great work of art? Or people who give up a well-paid job to carry out voluntary work in the Third World? No doubt the needs exist – but are they a hierarchy?

Many examination questions are possible based on these antecedents of marketing. The most likely would ask you to relate the theories to marketing problems: for example, a question might ask:

""What is the role of normative compliance in fashion marketing?""

The answer to this would begin by outlining normative compliance theory, then go on to discuss aspirational groups in the context of someone wishing to be part of a fashion-conscious group: the individual would not want to be part of the 'dork' group of unfashionable people, so a dissociative group might also come into the equation. In order to join the aspirational group, and leave the dissociative group, the consumer must conform to the norms of the aspirational group by buying fashionable clothes.

You may also be asked to discuss the development of marketing (see Thinking like a marketer section). For example:

""What is the difference between a product orientation and a production orientation?""

Product orientation is the view that the product should be 'the best'; in other words it should have all the features anyone could possibly want. This idea is flawed, because it means that people are paying for features they neither want nor need. The production orientation is the view that producing a standardised product at a low price is the best way forward: again, this is flawed because most people are prepared to pay a little extra to have a product which fits their needs exactly.

Textbook guide

ADCOCK, HALBORG AND ROSS: *Chapters 1 and 2.*
JOBBER: *Chapter 1.*
BRASSINGTON AND PETTITT: *Chapter 1.*
KOTLER, ARMSTRONG, SAUNDERS AND WONG: *Chapter 1.*
BLYTHE (2006): *Chapters 1 and 3.*

2	
the marketing environment	

The marketing environment can be divided in different ways, for the purpose of considering its effects on marketing planning: note, though, that the boundaries are extremely blurred.

The first division is between internal and external environments. The internal environment is about what happens inside the firm: the resources, attitudes, beliefs, structures and so forth within the firm. Corporate culture is particularly important: the shared beliefs and attitudes of the people who work for the organisation colour its decision-making. The external environment is everything outside the organisation: competitors, suppliers, customers, distributors, government departments, neighbours, and so on. These are included in marketing because of the **managing exchange** theme.

> *Note that many textbooks include customers/consumers in the external environment. This appears to be a contradiction of customer centrality.*

In recent years, the concept of internal and external environments has given way to stakeholder theory. Stakeholders are all the people and organisations which are impacted by, or impact on, the organisation. This way of looking at the environment removes the conceptual difficulty of placing customers outside the firm, but introduces the problem that customers are now regarded as only one influence among many (albeit a powerful one).

The marketing environment can also be divided into the macro environment, which is the set of conditions that affect every firm in the industry (and most firms outside the industry), and the micro-environment, which are the conditions that only affect the organisation itself. The macro-environment might include government departments, legal factors, the economic situation of the country, 'green' issues, technological change, political factors, and so forth.

Various texts (and indeed lecturers) have favourite ways of analysing the macro environment. The commonest ways of identifying the different factors are as follows:

1 **STEP:** this stands for Social, Technological, Economic and Political factors.

2 **STEEPLE:** this stands for Social, Technological, Economic, Ecological, Political, Legal, and Ethical factors.

3 **PESTLE:** Political, Economic, Social, Technological, Legal and Ecological factors.

Remember which of these your lecturer used, but do not ignore the others completely – mentioning one of the others will show that you have read around the subject.

Environmental scanning is about continually monitoring developments in each of the areas identified as being of importance to the firm. This might be carried out by line managers, by strategic planners, by a separate department, or by teams drawn from different parts of the company.

The micro environment is usually analysed using SWOT analysis. SWOT stands for Strengths, Weaknesses, Opportunities and Threats. Strengths and Weaknesses are mainly (though not entirely) about the internal environment of the firm, Opportunities and Threats are mainly (but again not entirely) about the external environment of the firm.

SWOT analysis is certainly not the whole picture, and it is probably nowhere near detailed enough for firms to base all their decisions on it. It also suffers from the major problem of being subjective – managers are not always entirely honest about their weaknesses, and disagree about what represent threats and opportunities. A more comprehensive approach to assessing the firm's position (at least as far as marketing conditions are concerned) is the marketing audit.

The marketing audit assesses the firm's marketing position under a comprehensive list of factors. The audit is intended to provide a snapshot of the firm's position. You are unlikely to be expected to remember the whole audit, but you might try to remember the main headings. These are as follows:

1 External audit:
- Macroenvironment.
- The market.
- Competition.

2 Internal audit:
- Operating results.
- Strategic issues.
- Marketing mix effectiveness.
- Marketing structures.
- Marketing systems.

All these analytical methods only provide a 'snapshot' of the firm's current position at the time of the analysis. This means that they are backward-looking: by the time a full marketing audit has been carried out, events have moved on and circumstances have changed.

 Taking it **FURTHER**

These analysis tools are widely-quoted: most textbooks and courses include them. Does industry use them, though? It seems like a lot of effort to go to for something which is out of date as soon as it happens. Also, the major problem is that most of the answers are decided on an arbitrary, subjective basis. The company's weaknesses might be seen as strengths by a different analyst, and the analysis itself does not tell us what to do about the situation, for which we have to use yet more arbitrary judgement. STEP, SWOT and the rest are not a magic wand – they are, at best, a guide for thinking about the problem.

You may well be asked how to use these analytical structures to analyse a case study (certainly you will if you take the Chartered Institute of

THE MARKETING ENVIRONMENT

Marketing examinations). In a standard exam situation, though, you are likely to be asked to critique the approach, perhaps as follows:

"What problems might arise for a company in the computer software industry when using STEEPLE analysis?"

The main problem for such a firm would be the volatility of the industry. Social and technological changes are rapid, and software companies must react swiftly to technological changes in hardware as well as social changes, such as an increased understanding of IT among the public at large. Political and legal forces are also at work, with major firms in the position of being able to lobby governments in order to affect legislation.

Alternatively, you may be asked to discuss the internal and external environments. For example:

"Many manufacturers of consumer goods allow their staff to buy products at a discount. Likewise, many firms have collaborative arrangements with other firms in the industry, even with competitors. How can these arrangements be considered in terms of environmental analysis?"

This question indicates that the division of the environment into internal/external or macro/micro may be artificial, because the arrangements described cross the boundaries. In the first case, employees are also customers, and in the second case competitors are also partners. An approach to resolving this would be to consider the parties separately in their separate roles, another approach would be to use stakeholder theory to analyse the specific needs of each group.

Textbook guide

ADCOCK, HALBORG AND ROSS: *Chapter 5.*
JOBBER: *Chapter 3.*
BRASSINGTON AND PETTITT: *Chapter 2.*
KOTLER, ARMSTRONG, SAUNDERS AND WONG: *Chapter 4.*
BLYTHE (2006): *Chapter 2.*

3	
consumer behaviour	

Consumer behaviour is one of the most important areas of marketing – not surprising, considering the emphasis on **customer centrality**. It often takes up more than one chapter in introductory marketing texts and may take up more than one lecture in your course. It certainly accounts for a large proportion of academic research.

Essentially, consumer behaviour is about people's decision-making about purchases, and the influences on those decisions. Understanding the processes involved helps with the **managing exchange** theme and also with the **segmentation** theme. The decision-making process which is most commonly quoted is the Engel, Kollat and Blackwell (EKB) model, which was first outlined in the 1960s. The EKB model is simple, and runs as follows:

1 **Problem recognition**: the consumer (or buyer) realises that there is a problem with the current assortment of goods he or she possesses.

2 **Information search**: this may be internal (based on what the person remembers) or external (based on information gained from friends, family, marketing communications such as brochures, the Internet, and so forth).

3 **Evaluation of alternatives**: choosing between the different products which might meet the need, and choosing one which provides the best fit.

4 **Purchase:** this is the actual exchange of money for goods.

5 **Post-purchase evaluation**: after using the product, the consumer is in a position to decide whether the decision was a correct one or not, and act accordingly.

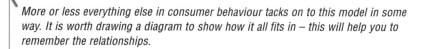

More or less everything else in consumer behaviour tacks on to this model in some way. It is worth drawing a diagram to show how it all fits in – this will help you to remember the relationships.

Problem recognition might come about from an internal stimulus (such as hunger, or thirst, or the realisation that the stereo is broken) or externally, which usually means a marketing-led activity such as an advertisement which shows a possible solution to a problem the consumer was not aware of until then.

The information search is crucial, because this is the second area in which consumer behaviour overlaps with marketing communications. The internal search can be influenced by advertisements or other communications which the individual remembers (or more importantly by direct positive experience with the product), and the external search can be influenced by advertising, brochures, websites, even by word of mouth facilitated by the marketers. The purpose of this activity is to ensure that the brand is part of the consumer's awareness set (the group of brands the consumer knows about). This is the main area in which learning and the **perception** running theme play a role.

Evaluation of alternatives involves the consumer in creating an **evoked set** (those brands which will be seriously considered before purchase). This is also called a **consideration set** – you may have been introduced to either of these terms, so use the one your lecturer prefers!

Purchase is the actual act of exchanging money for product. Where, when, and how this happens is (ultimately) the consumer's decision, so marketers need to anticipate the most favourable of the possibilities. This is the area where consumer behaviour overlaps into distribution (place) decisions. It is also the main area of **managing exchange**.

Post-purchase evaluation may result in consonance (being pleased with the product) or dissonance (being disappointed with the product). Either way, the evaluation forms part of the internal search, so future purchase decisions are affected. There is a considerable literature on both consonance and dissonance – complaining behaviour being one of the main issues involved.

Influences on the decision process mostly derive from the behavioural sciences covered earlier. To recap, social influences are:

- Culture.
- Social class.
- Geodemographics.
- Reference groups.

Personal influences are:

- Information processing (perception and learning).
- Motivation.

- Beliefs and attitudes.
- Personality.
- Lifestyle.
- Age and life cycle stage.

The buying situation also influences decision-making: people act differently when buying on the Internet than they do when buying in a retail store.

Problem-solving might be extensive, limited or habitual. Extensive problem-solving usually happens if the product is infrequently bought, is of high value, or is new to the consumer. It also happens sometimes when the consumer is highly-involved with the product, in other words if the product is very important to the consumer in terms of self-image, security, or emotional bond. There are four factors that affect **involvement**: these were identified by Laurent and Kapferer (1985), and are as follows:

1 Self-image.

2 **Perceived risk:** risk might be social (looking foolish), financial (wasting money) or physical (injury).

3 **Social factors:** the desire to belong to the right group, and be respected. Unlike risk, this is positive.

4 **Hedonic influences:** hedonism is about the pleasurable aspects of owning the product, or the 'fun' aspects.

Involvement is a concept you will often come across. Basically, it means that the consumer is emotionally attached to the brand, and will therefore buy no other. This is the holy grail for marketers!

Limited problem solving occurs when the customer is familiar with the product domain, namely the circumstances when the product will be used, but is less familiar with the actual product on offer.

Habitual problem-solving occurs when the customer is familiar with both the domain and the product.

For example, a beginner guitarist might spend a lot of time choosing a new guitar, as might a professional musician (because of the involvement issue). An experienced guitarist might spend some time on choosing new strings for a guitar if there is a new brand available (limited problem-solving) or might just buy the usual brand (habitual purchase).

Hedonic and **utilitarian** needs might also influence purchases. Hedonic factors relate to pleasure; utilitarian factors relate to practical aspects of the product. There is considerable overlap – a sales rep might need a comfortable car so as not to arrive at sales calls over-tired or irritable. This is where **customer centrality** helps us to think like the customer.

Remember that most products have features which relate to both hedonic needs and utilitarian needs. 'Hedonic' and 'utilitarian' refer to the needs of the consumer: the words do not describe the product.

Taking it **FURTHER**

Consumer behaviour is often portrayed as being very logical and mechanistic. In fact, people are more complex than this: they are often overtaken by impulse, often buy things based on an emotional reaction, and frequently buy things which are not good for them. Studies of consumer behaviour always look at people in the mass, usually segmenting them into similar groups. Although this makes for easy research, it ignores the diversity of people, who might be in one category one day and in a different category the next. For example, a man might be a careful family man taking out insurance to protect his family one day, but be a risk-taking dangerous sports enthusiast the next.

Categorising people is a risky business – as is predicting their behaviour! Unfortunately, we have to try to do it if we are to be able to plan ahead at all: but we should not imagine that we can really analyse consumer behaviour as clinically as we claimed to.

Examination questions on consumer behaviour vary widely, simply because there are so many issues involved. You will almost certainly be able to bring group influences and involvement into almost any question, so it is worthwhile to be confident about these even if the question does not appear to ask directly about them. For example, here is a sample question:

"What are the main factors to be taken into account when launching a new computer game?"

This appears to be a question about promotion issues and adoption of innovation (which is covered later, under Products). However, involvement will clearly be an issue for games aficionados, and especially young teenage players who are also subject to strong peer-group influences. Note that the above question might well appear in an examination on marketing communications or new-product development: don't forget that marketing subjects often overlap into each other!

Another possibility might be a question which addresses the decision-making process. For example,

"What decision-making steps would you expect someone to take if he or she were considering buying a DVD player? What influences might you expect him or her to be subject to?"

This is potentially a very large question. Buying a DVD player is an infrequent purchase, so the information search might be extended: the buyer might therefore be asking friends or family, and would therefore be subject to group influences from reference groups. Other influences would include marketing communications such as brochures, advertisements, and the salespeople in the shop.

Textbook guide

ADCOCK, HALBORG AND ROSS: *Chapter 6.*
JOBBER: *Chapter 3.*
BRASSINGTON AND PETTITT: *Chapter 3.*
KOTLER, ARMSTRONG, SAUNDERS AND WONG: *Chapter 6.*
BLYTHE (2006): *Chapter 6.*

4
business-to-business marketing

Business-to-business marketing (B2B) is actually much larger than business-to-consumer marketing in terms of size of markets. It is often virtually ignored in introductory marketing courses because lecturers think that students will relate better to examples taken from day-to-day life: we are all consumers, whereas relatively few of us are industrial buyers.

B2B is bigger than B2C because products typically pass through several firms before they reach the consumers. Each transfer from one firm to the next down the line is classified as part of B2B marketing, except the final sale to the consumers.

B2B is supposed to differ from B2C in that business buyers are thought to be more logical and professional in what they do. This is a dangerous assumption: business buyers are still human beings, and are likely to be swayed by a sales rep's personality or persuasive argument as much as anyone else. Many buyers also act impulsively at times, have good moods and bad moods, and of course make mistakes. This is relevant to the **managing exchange** running theme.

Here are the main differences between B2B and B2C:

1 *More decision-makers are involved.* The most common description of decision-makers is the Webster-Wind classification:

- Initiators, who first recognise the problem.
- Users, those who will use the product.
- Deciders, those who have real decision-making powers.
- Influencers, whose opinions are listened to but who are not directly involved.
- Buyers, who have the task of negotiating a final deal.
- Gatekeepers, who control the flow of information.

2 *Professional buyers:* in fact this can be misleading – although obviously industrial buyers are trained, and have great experience of buying within the product categories they deal with.

3 *Fewer buyers in most markets:* an industrial sales rep might only have 20 or 30 regular customers, whereas (say) a home-improvement salesman might meet hundreds of customers in a single year.

4 **Greater order sizes:** businesses buy in much larger quantities than do individual consumers.

5 **Demand** is derived from consumer markets, and fluctuates more as a result. If consumers are not buying, firms run their stocks down and so they buy less than usual; when demand picks up, they not only have to supply consumers, but they also build stocks again, so they buy even more than usual.

6 **Buying to specific requirements:** industrial buyers often work to a detailed specification of what the firm needs, and cannot be persuaded otherwise: for example, if a buyer is sourcing components for a machine, they will have to fit with other components.

7 **Risks:** decision-makers risk more than just the money involved; they also risk their careers, or even their jobs.

8 **Negotiation** tends to be much more common. Negotiations may be about price, specifications, delivery, quantity, or payment terms.

9 **Reciprocal buying:** in some cases, firms are able to negotiate a deal whereby the selling firm agrees to buy some of the end product from the buying firm. This type of deal is sometimes regarded as unethical, and can be illegal if an abuse of power is involved (this is the case in the United States, for example).

> *If you are using an American textbook, you may find that the chapter on Ethics (which is a requirement of all US marketing textbooks) will contain issues which would not be regarded as unethical elsewhere, and may omit others which non-Americans would regard as unethical.*

Much of the attention in B2B marketing is given to the industrial buyer and his or her behaviour. This goes to the **customer centrality** theme. The buying situation (buy class, as it is also called) may be in one of three categories:

1 **Straight rebuy:** this happens when the product is purchased regularly, and this is simply a repeat order.

2 **Modified rebuy:** this happens when there is some change to the usual order, either in quantity or in specification.

3 **New task:** this happens when the product is totally new to the company, and therefore involves the most time and negotiation.

The buy class affects the composition of the decision-making unit, the length of the decision process, and the negotiation level. From the marketer's viewpoint, it is important to become involved with the decision-making as early as possible in order to manage both the **customer perception** and the **exchange process**.

> *If you are asked, for example, to explain how you would approach a buyer in a new-task buy class, remember that initiators and influencers are more important in the early stages of new-task buying. Buyers come in much later, when the specifications are drawn up – by which time it is usually too late!*

Incidentally, it is worth noting that the members of the decision-making unit are not necessarily mutually exclusive – a user can also be an influencer, or a gatekeeper can be an initiator, for example.

In recent years, there have been many changes in purchasing practice which have affected marketers. It is worthwhile understanding purchasing methods and philosophies, because this will make it easier to formulate marketing approaches, and **manage the exchange**. The key changes are:

1 **Just-in-time purchasing:** this aims to minimise stocks by ensuring that deliveries are made as nearly as possible to the point at which the goods will be needed.

2 **Centralised purchasing:** this is used by large firms so that buyers can specialise in buying particular types of product.

3 **Reverse marketing:** here the buyer initiates the process, proactively seeking out firms, using a 'shopping list' of specifications, delivery requirements and prices and seeking to persuade suppliers to meet the criteria if they want the business. This approach takes the initiative away from the supplier, and works well in situations where there is an oversupply.

4 **Leasing:** instead of buying capital equipment outright, firms often lease equipment, paying a rental instead of a lump sum. This saves capital, but also gives firms an important tax advantage.

Relationships are likely to be longer-term and deeper between firms than they are between a firm and consumers. There is more on relationship marketing later in the book.

Most introductory marketing courses do not go into much detail on B2B marketing, and many textbooks simply tack it onto the consumer behaviour chapter. There is a trend towards having dedicated courses in B2B marketing, however, as lecturers realise that most marketing in the real world is, in fact, B2B.

Taking it **FURTHER**

Industrial markets are characterised by derived demand. This means that the ultimate consumer drives the production, and therefore the buying, throughout the B2B process. This gives us a problem when we talk about customer centrality, because supplier firms might be faced with a conflict between supplying what the immediate customer wants, and supplying the best product for the ultimate consumer. For example, a manufacturer might want to build in some obsolescence (produce something with a fixed lifespan so that the company can sell more product in future). This is clearly not in the end consumer's best interests. On the other hand, the intention is to create a demand and generate profits, not simply to please the consumers at all costs.

Exam questions in B2B marketing tend to be simplistic, because the subject is usually only covered in a fairly superficial way. For example, you might be asked to define the roles of the decision-making unit (DMU), or explain how you would go about launching a product. Of course, the concept of the DMU might not apply in some cases, notably in reverse marketing. Here are two sample exam questions.

❝ What might be the role of a company's auditor in the purchase of a new computer system? What are the marketing implications of this? ❞

An auditor has the task of verifying the company's accounts, for tax purposes and for protection of shareholders. An auditor would probably have the role of influencer, and may even have the role of user as well, but would not be a decider, buyer, or initiator. It is possible that an auditor would be a gatekeeper, helping to filter out irrelevant information.

The marketing implications are that it would be as well to involve the auditor in the early stages of the discussions. A conversation with the accounts department of the company should include the auditor, although it is probably better to speak to the auditor separately, and as early as possible in order to establish the selling company's position with someone who is a powerful influencer. This gives a good opportunity to cut out competitors.

❝What difficulties might a sales representative meet with in dealing with industrial buyers, as opposed to dealing with consumers?❞

The main problem a sales representative has is that industrial buying involves more than one decision-maker, in most cases. This means that the sales representative will have the task of identifying the members of the DMU and approaching them with the proposition.

Sales representatives are also up against professional buyers who have been trained in handling sales people. They tend to take a more considered and less emotional approach to buying, and will probably be better negotiators.

Textbook guide

ADCOCK, HALBORG AND ROSS: *Chapter 7.*
JOBBER: *Chapter 4.*
BRASSINGTON AND PETTITT: *Chapter 4.*
KOTLER, ARMSTRONG, SAUNDERS AND WONG: *Chapter 7.*
BLYTHE (2006): *Chapters 5, 11 and 17.*

5	
segmentation and targeting	

Segmentation is the process of dividing the market up into smaller groups, with similar needs. Segmentation can be done by breaking down a large market, or by building up from individual customers. For a segment to be viable, it needs the following characteristics:

1 *It must be definable.*

2 *It must be sizeable* – large enough to be worth serving. This implies that the segment must be measurable.

3 *It must be reachable* – there must be a promotional medium which reaches the segment.

4 *It must be relevant.*

5 *It should be homogeneous.* This means that the members should have similar needs in terms of what the company has to offer.

A problem for the student is that different authors use different terminology for these factors, and may omit some of them or add others. Broadly, the way to think of a segment is that it represents a group of ideal customers. If, as a marketer, you can develop a detailed mental image of the kind of customer your product will appeal to, the rest of the marketing planning becomes much simpler.

Markets can be segmented in a number of ways. The most common ones (not necessarily in order of usefulness) for consumer markets are:

- Age.
- Family life stage.
- Geography.
- Gender.
- Income.

- Social class.
- Ethnicity.
- Lifestyle.
- Attitudes.
- Behaviour.

- Benefits sought.
- Loyalty.
- Stage in buying process.
- Use occasion.
- Frequency of purchase.

There is a very real danger of mistaking the true segmentation basis. For example, a market might appear to segment by age, but in fact segment by behaviour: an example is the nightclub market, which used to be thought of as a youth market until the rising divorce rate put many older single people back in circulation. Nightclubs are, in fact, a singles market, part of the mating game – age is a red herring!

There are, of course, other possibilities. In B2B markets, the commonest bases are:

- Geography.
- Industry.
- Size of firm.

- Purchase frequency.
- Benefits sought.

Again, there are others.

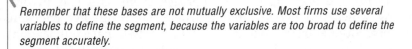

Remember that these bases are not mutually exclusive. Most firms use several variables to define the segment, because the variables are too broad to define the segment accurately.

International segmentation follows much the same process, but with the added proviso that some segments cross national boundaries. Such global segments are currently relatively few in number, because cultural differences tend to interfere, but there is certainly a global youth market (driven by MTV and the fashion industry), and a global 'jet-set executive' market.

Some segmentation bases can mislead marketers. A classic example is segmentation by ethnicity. In Britain and many other countries with sizeable immigrant populations, the boundaries have become extremely blurred: one cannot say with absolute confidence that only West Indians will buy West Indian foods, for example. Certainly Indian food has overtaken British food as the most popular restaurant meal. Even clothing and musical instruments have been disseminated among the population at large. This is about **customer centrality** – looking at what consumers actually do, rather than who their ancestors are!

The reason for segmenting the market is to make the best use of the firm's resources. There are no longer any products that please everybody – consumers have become too discerning. Even products such as Coca-Cola have a minority share of the markets in which they operate. In any case, most firms could not afford the kind of resources implied in promoting their products to everyone – the cost would be astronomical. Firms therefore divide up the market, then target the segments which appear most promising first.

The segment which appears best to target is not necessarily the most profitable one or the richest one. It may be that a small firm will target a less profitable segment in order to avoid head-to-head confrontation with a larger firm.

Segmenting is a crucial concept in marketing, because it defines the company's position in the market. Targeting is the next stage following on from segmentation: targeting is about choosing the most appropriate segments and deciding how to approach them. This may involve choosing which product to offer; it will certainly involve choosing which promotional platform to use, and it is likely to have implications for distribution. In fact, all the marketing mix decisions flow from the targeting decision.

Targeting allows the firm to use different strategies for each segment it targets. Most firms target several segments at once, because this offers a more secure situation. If one segment fails, another will keep the company afloat. You may well be asked to segment a given market, especially in a case-study based question: you should be able to decide which segments to target, and justify your decision.

> *Choosing which segments to target implies rejection of other segments. Some marketers go to considerable trouble to ensure that 'undesirable' customers do NOT buy the firm's products – this is especially the case in the insurance and entertainment industries. Pubs and nightclubs do not want rowdy customers, and insurance companies do not want people who are likely to make claims. You will gain marks if you can show how to get rid of undesirables!*

Positioning is linked to targeting. Positioning is where the company stands relative to competitors, in the mental map of its target segments. This is about the **perception** theme. Positioning is likely to be multidimensional, i.e. it is measured against several variables. One of these will almost certainly be cost, another will be quality, and others might include reliability, brand image, service quality, or product range. Marketers need to decide which factors are crucial in the minds of the target segment, and position accordingly.

> *Note that marketers should look for target groups whose needs are not being met fully by existing suppliers, then supply something which fits the need. This implies that marketers should be doing things which the competitors are not doing – copying competitors is the last refuge of the incompetent!*

Repositioning the firm or its products means changing the perceptual map of the consumers. This may only mean reminding people of the importance of a product feature they already know exists, or it may mean informing them of a new product feature. It may even mean drawing comparisons with other products, not necessarily in the same industry: calling your product 'the Rolls Royce of …' or (in the USA) 'the Cadillac of … ' positions the product quickly in people's minds.

> *Consumers do not believe that they will get top quality and low price together. People go for value for money – which is a subjective concept that develops from beliefs about quality relative to price.*

Positioning messages need to be clear, consistent, competitive, and credible.

Taking it *FURTHER*

Segmenting markets is a key concept in marketing, but it has to be said that people often shift from one segment to another. Changes in financial circumstances (for example, a pay rise or, conversely, a redundancy) can move an individual from one group to another fairly rapidly. What's more, the individual's tastes and preferences will remain the same for some time. A street sweeper who wins the lottery is still likely to prefer beer to champagne, and sausages to caviar. Conversely, a company director who is ousted by the Board is likely to take some time to adjust to a much lower income, and will still try to maintain a high standard of living.

Realistically, can we actually segment effectively in a world of rapid changes? Might it not be better simply to offer the products as widely as possible, and let the market segment itself? After all, our company director might occasionally enjoy fish and chips out of a newspaper, and our street sweeper might well enjoy an occasional night in a luxury hotel.

Exam questions on segmentation often revolve around the reasons for segmenting. Here are two examples:

“What are the advantages of segmenting markets? In what circumstances might you NOT segment a market, namely treat the market as if it were one segment, susceptible to a single marketing mix? ”

In answering this question, you should begin by listing the advantages of segmentation (resource efficiency, improved targeting, differentiated marketing) and discuss each one. You should also mention the advantages of keeping out the 'undesirables' – customers who are more trouble than they are worth, for whatever reason. You would treat a market as a single segment if it turned out that it was impossible to segment, perhaps because no segments could be identified. You might also do this if the product genuinely has a near-universal appeal – for example, cleaning fluids or supermarkets. Such examples are extremely rare, though.

"How would you segment the market for nightclubs?"

This question offers many possibilities for discussion. It is tempting to segment by age, but in fact nightclubs are popular with single people (who are mostly young, admittedly). Most nightclubs probably segment by age (demographically) but it might be better to segment by life stage (single as opposed to married) or by lifestyle ('party animal' types as opposed to 'intellectual' types). Behavioural segmentation (people who like to stay out late) may also be a factor. In practice, of course, the market should be segmented by several variables in order to narrow down to a specific audience.

Textbook guide

ADCOCK, HALBORG AND ROSS: *Chapter 8.*
JOBBER: *Chapter 7.*
BRASSINGTON AND PETTITT: *Chapter 5.*
KOTLER, ARMSTRONG, SAUNDERS AND WONG: *Chapters 9 and 10.*
BLYTHE (2006): *Chapter 6.*

6	
marketing information and research	

Marketing research follows on naturally from segmentation, because it is the means by which firms identify segments. In some courses it is taught before segmentation; in others it is taught afterwards, depending on whether the lecturer believes that topics should be taught in the order in which they occur in the real world, or in an order which makes them easier to teach. In some cases, lecturers will concentrate on telling you how to commission marketing research from a specialist agency; this approach is growing more common, because unless you are studying a specific named marketing degree course, you are more likely to commission research than to carry it out. Nevertheless, it helps to have an understanding of how it is done, even if you are paying someone else to do the actual work.

Research comes from two main sources: **secondary research** and **primary research**. Secondary research comes from published sources, and has usually been collected for some other purpose: primary research is original research, carried out for a specific decision-making purpose.

If you think of secondary research as second-hand research, it makes it easier to remember which is which.

Secondary research should always be done first, because there is no point in re-inventing the wheel: if someone has already researched something relevant to the topic, it is cheaper, quicker and easier to read their research than to carry out your own. It may sound paradoxical to think of secondary research as the first to carry out, and primary research as the second, but if you follow the tip above it makes more sense! Research methods can be categorised as follows:

1 *Marketing information systems* offer continuous streams of information, often including the environmental scanning systems discussed under the marketing environment above. MkIS also includes internal data such as sales records, profitability of specific products, or (better) profitability of market segments.

This is an example of customer centrality in action. Firms should not assess the profitability of products if they are customer-centred: they should assess the profitability of groups of customers. Yet many fail to do so.

2   *Ad hoc research:* this is research carried out for a specific purpose: it might involve primary or secondary research, and probably both.

3   *Continuous research:* like a marketing information system, continuous research is a regular update on what the company needs to know.

There are many ways of carrying out primary research, but they can be divided into qualitative and quantitative methods. **Quantitative** methods typically involve surveys, and are intended to provide information such as '27 per cent of consumers use bleach in their toilets every day' or '56 per cent of coffee drinkers prefer ground coffee to instant coffee'. Quantitative research therefore produces quantities. **Qualitative** research is better for telling us *why* 56 per cent of coffee drinkers prefer ground coffee, but actually drink instant coffee most of the time. Qualitative research uses focus groups or in-depth interviews with people to find out what their attitudes are and how they are formed. It therefore tells us about the qualities of the problem. It also helps in assessing **consumer perception** of brands.

In the real world, incidentally, qualitative research is proving to be more useful, because it is often more reliable and it gives a better understanding of how consumers form their ideas.

You are very likely to be asked about the advantages and disadvantages of each of these types of research. If you remember that quantitative research is good for telling us *what* happened, and qualitative research is good for telling us *why* it happened, you should be able to keep those advantages and disadvantages clear.

Qualitative research (in the form of focus groups) became fashionable with political parties after the famous Gallup polls (which are quantitative) failed to predict the outcomes of three UK general elections in a row.

The research process runs as follows:

1   *Research planning:* identify the problem, develop a research brief, produce a research proposal.

2 *Exploratory research:* secondary research, consultation with experts, observation, possibly some qualitative research to determine the dimensions of the problem.

3 *Data collection:* in many cases, this will be a survey; a sample of the population will be taken, and a questionnaire or interview conducted. An experiment might be conducted (for example, test marketing in a particular area).

4 Data analysis and interpretation.

Analysis is not the same as interpretation. Analysis is rearranging the data so that it provides information; interpretation is about telling us what it means.

5 Report writing and presentation.

Common qualitative techniques are:

1 *In-depth interview:* people are recruited to give their opinions, and are allowed to speak fairly freely about the topic area. Sometimes the interviews are structured (specific questions are asked), sometimes they are semi-structured (topics of interest are mentioned to them) and sometimes they are unstructured (they are allowed to talk freely about anything provided it is about the topic of the research).

2 *Focus group:* a group of people are brought together to discuss the topic between them. This has the advantage that they often trigger ideas from each other. It has the disadvantage that sometimes the most vociferous members drown out the opinions of the more timid members.

3 *Consultation with experts:* this could be in the form of the in-depth interview, or could be a **DELPHI** process in which experts give their opinions, the opinions are circulated to the group, who then adapt their responses. The process is repeated until consensus is reached.

4 *Observation:* watching how people behave, for example, in shopping malls or supermarkets. This has the advantage that the personality of the researcher will not affect the behaviour.

5 **Experiment:** this is a controlled observation: the subject is given a stimulus (for example, shown an advertisement) and his or her reactions are noted.

All these methods rely on an objective researcher to analyse the results: interpreting what happened will differ according to who is doing the interpreting.

In any research, a key issue is to decide who to include in the research. It is clearly impossible to include the whole population, so researchers usually take samples. This can lead to bias in the results. Other sources of bias come from the following:

1 Poorly-designed questionnaires, containing leading questions.

2 **Interviewer bias:** the interviewer accidentally (or sometimes deliberately) says or does something which leads the respondent to answer in a particular way.

 Taking it **FURTHER**

One of the current debates in academic research (as opposed to commercial research) is whether any research can be conducted objectively. The argument runs that any researcher begins with a set of prejudices, or at least comes from a cultural background, which dictates the way the research is conducted. Therefore there is an automatic source of bias.

This argument has considerable merit, but leaves us with a problem: do we therefore assume that all research is biased? Or do we simply accept that the researcher may have a viewpoint, but that it is valid in the context of the research? Or do we do our honest best as researchers to 'tune out' this type of bias?

You are likely to be asked to explain the advantages and disadvantages of different research techniques. These are outlined in your textbook: you might also be asked to recommend a research procedure for a given problem. Here is a sample question.

"Your company sells vitamin-rich health foods aimed at recovering invalids. How would you research the possibilities for repositioning the product for the slimming market?"

The relative sizes of the slimming market and the invalid market could probably be determined from secondary research, but the possibilities for repositioning would require primary research. First, you would need to determine what people's existing perceptions of the product are, if this information is not already available internally or from published surveys. This would probably be best conducted using qualitative research such as focus groups or depth interviews. You will need to explain the advantages and disadvantages of each. Second, you might conduct a survey to determine whether the views expressed in the focus group are widespread, sampling from people who are overweight and trying to slim. Finally you would need to analyse and interpret the data, probably using tests of significance. Note that this question needs **customer centrality, perception,** and **segmentation** themes!

And another question:

"What are the advantages and disadvantages of qualitative research as opposed to quantitative research? When would you choose one rather than the other?"

The first half of this question is straightforward because it is descriptive. All you need to do is learn explanations in the book and repeat them. The second part is more difficult, because it calls for judgement: basically, you would use quantitative research to find out what has happened, and qualitative research to find out why it happened. A good way to gain extra marks is to point out that the two methods are not mutually exclusive: good research would quite probably include both approaches.

Textbook guide

ADCOCK, HALBORG AND ROSS: *Chapter 9.*
JOBBER: *Chapter 6.*
BRASSINGTON AND PETTITT: *Chapter 6.*
KOTLER, ARMSTRONG, SAUNDERS AND WONG: *Chapter 8.*
BLYTHE (2006): *Chapter 7.*

7

marketing communication theories

Marketing communication is, not surprisingly, the most visible part of marketing, and is therefore often assumed to be the whole of marketing by non-marketers. For many students, it is also often the most interesting: it overlaps a great deal with consumer behaviour, because it impacts on the information-processing activities of people and it has an input at every stage of the decision process. Therefore it goes to the **customer perception** running theme. A large amount of marketing communications is aimed at reminding people about a need, or helping them to recognise a problem: an even greater amount is aimed at informing and persuading people so that the brand is included in the evoked set and (with luck) in the consideration set.

Most courses teach the Schramm model of communications. This shows a transmitter, a receiver, encoding of an intelligent message and decoding of it by the receiver, with interference and noise distorting the message. Sometimes the model also includes reference to the sender's and receiver's fields of experience, and to feedback loops which confirm that the message has been correctly received. This model has been around for 50 years, and provides a reasonable working model, but it has been criticised on the grounds that human beings are not radios: the receiver (in this case) thinks about the message and interprets it, and also adds the message to previous information about the company and brand in order to extract meaning. This is very much about **customer centrality**; customers are active, not passive.

You may be asked to describe the model, in which case it is worthwhile to remember the diagram from your textbook and reproduce it. You should gain extra marks if, as well as describing it, you also mention the criticisms outlined above.

Marketing communications are often divided into the promotional mix, as follows:

1 *Advertising:* this is defined as the paid insertion of a message in a medium.

2 *Personal selling:* this is any direct person-to-person communication.

3 *Public relations:* this is any general communications intended to improve the public image of brands or companies.

4 *Sales promotion:* this is any activity intended to generate a temporary boost in sales.

> The barriers between the elements of the promotional mix are far from fixed, and there is even some debate about whether sales promotion and personal selling belong in the mix at all.

There are now several new techniques which deserve inclusion in the marketing mix. These are:

1 Internet and online marketing.

2 Direct marketing (telephone selling, mailings, etc.).

3 SMS marketing (texting of messages to mobile phones).

4 *Ambient advertising* – messages on T-shirts, on stair risers, on petrol pumps, and so forth.

No doubt other techniques will appear as time goes by.

Usually, the promotional mix is taught as are ingredients in a recipe. The ingredients must be added at the right times, and in the right quantities, if the recipe is to work; also, one ingredient cannot be substituted for another. This view of the marketing mix has led to the concept of integrated marketing communications, or IMC. A key writer about IMC is Professor Philip Kitchen.

The argument behind IMC is that, as the number of elements in the promotional mix grows, there is an increased risk of consumers receiving different messages from each medium. IMC is an attempt to ensure that all communications from the company tell the same story.

In practice this is remarkably hard to achieve, because the medium is also part of the message: a newspaper advertisement conveys a different image according to whether it is in a quality newspaper or a cheap tabloid, never mind whether it is in a newspaper or in a SMS text.

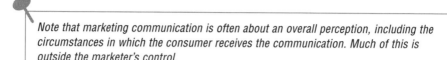

> Note that marketing communication is often about an overall perception, including the circumstances in which the consumer receives the communication. Much of this is outside the marketer's control.

For IMC to work, the company needs to recognise every point at which the brand and the consumer interact. This means that companies need to ensure that every impression anyone receives of the brand is not only positive, but also reflects the brand's values. Some less obvious examples are as follows:

1 Signs on the company's delivery vehicles saying 'How's my driving?' with a freephone number give a good impression of the company.

2 Employees go home after work, and often talk about the company. Whether or not they give a good account of the firm is part of internal marketing communications.

3 Corporate headquarters (and branch offices) need to give the right impression.

4 Sales people (and their cars) should be appropriate, and fit the brand image.

These examples are useful in exam situations, because they indicate the difficulty of ensuring that all communications from the company are consistent.

Maintaining a level of consistency in communications starts by ensuring that all the employees in the organisation understand the basic corporate message, and live it. In many cases, companies achieve this by having a simple corporate slogan (Avis's 'We're number two, so we try harder' or Tesco's 'Every little helps' are good examples to use).

> Remember that integrated marketing communication is an academic concept. Although many firms try to utilise it, few have achieved truly integrated campaigns.

Finally, when planning a campaign managers need to set the budget. There are five methods for doing this, as follows:

1 *Objective and task method:* this involves deciding what the objectives of the campaign arc, what tasks need to be carried out to achieve the objectives, and therefore what the tasks will cost. This is an extremely difficult calculation to make with any accuracy.

2 *Percentage of sales:* this method sets the promotional budget as a percentage of sales. It is based on the false idea that sales create promotion: if sales fall, promotion will reduce, which means that sales fall even further and so forth.

3 *Comparative parity:* here the budget is matched to that of the competitors: in effect, the firm's marketing budget is being set by its competitors.

A common rule of thumb: if the firm wants to capture 20 per cent of a market, it needs to spend about 25 per cent of the total promotional expenditure by competitors already in the market.

4 *Marginal approach:* the marketer spends up to the point where further expenditure will not bring in enough new business to justify the expenditure. This is virtually impossible to calculate.

5 *All-you-can-afford:* this is probably the most common in most firms. The company spends whatever it can spare from other activities, which means that the marketing department fights for its budget against other departments.

You may be asked to contrast the different budgeting methods. Each has its drawbacks, and the two with the best conceptual justification (objective and task, and marginal approaches) are almost impossible to calculate in practice. Calculating the return on marketing communications is notoriously difficult, because too many factors are involved.

Marketing communications can only be measured against communications objectives (brand awareness, corporate image, and so on) not against marketing objectives (increased market share, loyalty, repeat purchase). This makes valuing the marketing communications effort extremely difficult.

Integrating marketing communication is difficult, but is an ideal worth striving for.

Taking it **FURTHER**

The Schramm model of communications is the most widely-taught model, but does it really describe what happens in the real world? It appears to be extremely mechanistic, and in fact does not accord with more recent thinking on communications. For example, Mantovani (1996) maintains that communication is a way of developing a mutually acceptable view of the world. Each party to the communication adds something to the common view, and takes something away, so that communication is a joint effort, not something instigated by a transmitter and passively accepted by a receiver. Deetz (1992) adds to this by suggesting that many, if not most, communications are intended not to convey information, but to produce an effect in the receiver. These communications, which Deetz calls political communications, are certainly the kind of communications most marketers produce.

If this view is correct, the Schramm model is naïve to say the least. In any case, most marketing texts ignore issues such as miscommunication, misunderstanding, and deliberate deception (except in the chapters on ethical marketing).

Exam questions based on general marketing communications principles are likely to require you to use the Schramm model of communications and apply it in some way. For example:

"How might you minimise the bad effects of interference and noise when planning a campaign for an insurance company?"

The more direct the campaign, the less chance there is of interference and (to an extent) noise. Also, feedback (interactivity) will reduce the bad effects when noise or interference do occur. Using an integrated campaign which uses several media increases the chance of the message getting through intact: a direct element such as the Internet, direct mail or telemarketing will cut through some of the clutter, but of course some direct media have extremely low response rates.

For integrated marketing communications, you might be asked something along the lines of:

"What are the benefits and problems of integrating a marketing communications campaign?"

Integrating the campaign has the advantage of reinforcing the message and also maximising the chances that the message will be received. It has the major drawback that it is actually extremely difficult to separate out the message from the medium: a message sent via a tabloid newspaper has a different meaning from one sent via an advertisement on television. It is also difficult to achieve in practice because there is rarely a single message. In most cases, there are several messages which a company sends out, from several internal sources.

Textbook guide

ADCOCK, HALBORG AND ROSS: *Chapter 15.*
JOBBER: *Chapter 12.*
BRASSINGTON AND PETTITT: *Chapter 14.*
KOTLER, ARMSTRONG, SAUNDERS AND WONG: *Chapter 18.*
BLYTHE (2006): *Chapter 8.*

8	
branding and brand management	

The **brand** is the coordinating device for all marketing activities. It gives customers a 'shorthand' way of remembering what the product is, and what it does, which helps with the perceptual process since it allows customers to 'pigeonhole' the brand within their perceptual map. This is, of course, relevant to the **customer perception** running theme.

It may help to think of the brand as a lens, through which marketers focus their efforts and consumers view the product.

The brand should be seen as an investment vehicle. Communication activities aimed at raising the profile of the brand, or raising its status in the eyes of customers, will pay off over a number of years (incidentally, this is an issue which marketers often find themselves fighting over in management meetings. Finance directors and others often have a much shorter-term view of promotional campaigns).

Branding terminology covers a number of different types of brand strategy. Here are the main terms:

- Manufacturer brands, or proprietary brands: these are the brands owned by the manufacturer of the products. Manufacturer brands subdivide into family line branding (where one brand covers a number of products, for example, Heinz 57), and discrete branding, where each product has its own brand. Sometimes there may be a combination of the two – Homepride Cook-In Sauces, for example. A recent development has been so-called fighter brands, which are low-price brands introduced by manufacturers to combat supermarket 'value' brands.
- Own-label brands (distributor brands) are owned by the retailer: again these may subdivide into generic brands which cover a wide range of products (for example, Tesco's Finest) or may simply carry the name of the retailer.
- Co-branding: two companies offering complementary products join together to offer a joint product (for example, Häagen Dazs and Bailey's offering Bailey's flavour ice cream).
- Global branding: using the same brand name worldwide.

Branding makes a big difference to customer perception of the product. A famous example is the Pepsi vs. Coca-Cola taste tests. If people taste the products without knowing which is which, they mainly prefer Pepsi: if they can see the brand name on each, they prefer the Coke.

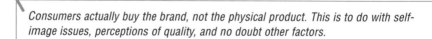

Consumers actually buy the brand, not the physical product. This is to do with self-image issues, perceptions of quality, and no doubt other factors.

Branding is a way of positioning the product against other products on the market. The brand adds to the core product, which is usually similar to other products on the market. For example, small cars offer much the same benefits and features, but the brand makes the difference because it conveys an impression of a particular style, or qualities such as reliability. Manufacturers use the brand to convey the image that most suits their strategy – Volkswagen emphasises reliability, Citroën emphasises fun, Renault emphasises stylishness. The core product is a box on wheels for transporting people and luggage: the augmented (branded) product is something extra.

You need to remember that brands are much more than just a name, but of course the name counts for a lot because it conveys the brand's personality.

> *Brands are often considered in terms of a personality – the BBC is widely known as Auntie, because this is what the brand conveys: a somewhat staid, reliable, comfortable person who looks after us without being critical.*

Sometimes companies extend the brand, which means they apply the same brand to other products (often products which bear no relationship to the original product). Examples include Harley-Davidson, who have extended their motorcycle brand to a clothing range, and of course the Virgin brand, which covers everything from recording artists to railways to airlines. Virgin seem able to extend the brand indefinitely, but most companies hit problems when they try this. This is because the **customer perception** of the brand becomes clouded.

Brands may need to be repositioned as their customers mature or as market conditions change. You may be asked to consider how to reposition a brand, in which case it is worth remembering that brands act as a focus for the organisation as well as the public. If everyone (including, but not only, the marketers) in the organisation has the same view of the brand, the image will be propagated successfully.

> *It will look better in your exams if you can think of some examples of repositioned brands yourself rather than use the same old tired ones out of the textbooks.*

Rebranding (changing the brand name and/or image) is a risky procedure, but is a common occurrence. The reasons are as follows:

- Merger or acquisition: the new company has a new name, and a new identity, so the corporate brand needs to change.

- Desire to reposition or create a new image: rather than try to change people's view of the old brand name, it may be easier simply to choose a new name and image. This happened to Townsend Thoresen Ferries following the Zeebrugge disaster in which almost 200 people died: the company rebranded as P&O Ferries.
- Sale or acquisition of parts of a business.
- Corporate strategy changes: if the company moves into new areas, the old brand may conflict with this and need to be changed.
- Brand familiarity: the product brand may take over from the corporate brand in people's minds.
- International marketing: harmonising brand names across national boundaries creates economies of scale in promotion, and clarity for people who travel a lot (hence Marathon became Snickers, and Jif became Cif).
- Consolidation of brands within a national boundary: again, this is about economies of scale.
- Legal problems: sometimes the brand name is or becomes illegal in some markets.

Changing a brand name requires careful planning and equally careful implementation. In some cases, the process takes place over a number of years so that customers have time to get used to the transition.

You will need to consider the whole situation from the customer's viewpoint, of course. How do customers actually recognise the brand? It is unlikely to be solely from the name – design and colour of the packaging is a more immediate cue, since people scan supermarket shelves too quickly to read the name on the package. This is another issue in **customer centrality** – we look at what people actually do!

> *If you are changing a brand, it is probably a good idea not to change everything at once. Changing the name first, and the packaging design later and gradually, will probably be more effective than doing it the other way round.*

Brand managers are often recruited direct from university: it is a common starting-point for a marketing career. Brand managers are responsible for every aspect of marketing a particular brand, so it is worthwhile gaining a good understanding of how branding works.

Branding can be viewed as a way of controlling markets. Big brand owners such as Nike do not make anything – all the actual manufacture is subcontracted to cheap labour factories in the Far East. Nike merely manages the brand, and does so in such a way that it seeks to exclude other companies such as Adidas from its markets. It also concentrates wealth and power in already-rich countries.

Coca-Cola, McDonald's, Microsoft and many others actually offer products which are no better (and may be worse) than their rivals, but have established their brands in people's minds. To test this, try taking a child to Burger King instead of McDonald's and see what happens!

There is a question over whether branding is manipulative of consumers and therefore unethical. Certainly some consumers appear entirely brand driven, whereas others are brand switchers, buying the one with the best offer on at present, or the one which comes readily to hand. Furthermore, some consumers are brand driven for some products and not for others. Obviously consumers are exercising choice, and are being seen to do so.

For the typical exam question on branding, you need to remember that the brand is a shorthand device, and has a personality, and this is what customers buy rather than a physical product. Managing the brand may be a firm's only activity. Here are some sample questions:

"Under what circumstances would you consider consolidating brand names?"

There are several circumstances: first, if consumers' perception of one or more of the brands has become negative; second, if one or more of the brands is in a market which is likely to decline, or if the brands need repositioning for other reasons; third, if corporate strategy has shifted so that consolidation is more viable.

In answering this question more fully, you should expand on the effects on consumers and outline problems which will arise in terms of re-establishing the brands in people's perceptions.

"Why is a brand sometimes considered to be an investment vehicle?"

This question addresses an issue which is commonly identified in marketing: finance directors tend to think of marketing expenditure as a cost, whereas marketers think of it as an investment. The brand has a value in itself (sometimes referred to in the accounts as 'goodwill') so expenditure on promoting the brand and positioning it appropriately can actually appear on the balance sheet, as an asset, rather than in the profit and loss account as a cost.

Textbook guide

ADCOCK, HALBORG AND ROSS: *Chapter 12.*
JOBBER: *Chapter 8.*
BRASSINGTON AND PETTITT: *Chapter 7.*
KOTLER, ARMSTRONG, SAUNDERS AND WONG: *Chapter 13.*
BLYTHE (2006): *Chapters 3 and 8.*

9	
international marketing	

During the last 30 years or so, world trade has multiplied manifold. The drivers for this are as follows:

1 Governments have recognised that trade is always beneficial — both parties gain from exchanges. Trade barriers have therefore been reduced dramatically.

2 Transportation systems have improved tremendously: apart from the rise in commercial aviation, surface shipping has become several times more efficient.

3 Firms have grown too big for their domestic markets.

4 Global markets have emerged as a result of mass communications and movement of populations.

Remember that internationalisation works both ways – more foreign firms are entering UK markets, so no firm can escape from international competition.

International marketing is giving way to **global** marketing: the difference is that internationalisation refers to trading abroad, perhaps in several countries, whereas globalisation means trading with the world as a whole, and seeking out markets which may be national, or which may cross national borders.

World trade has been steadily liberalised since the end of the Second World War (largely because trade makes war less likely – one does not shoot the grocer). Many firms have outgrown their domestic markets and moved overseas. At the same time, raw materials shortages have led to firms looking further afield for supplies, and even for labour.

Two main theories dominate the internationalisation of the firm: first, the stages of development theory (sometimes also called the Uppsala theory, after the university where it was first formulated) states that firms move through a series of stages in becoming truly international. Beginning with exporting, the firm moves through establishing a sales office overseas, then establishing a warehouse, then manufacturing, and finally becoming truly multinational by allowing the overseas sub-sidiaries to exercise a large degree of autonomy. The competing theory is Dunning's Eclectic Theory (1993), which says that firms move into overseas markets by the means which most readily suit their strengths. There is evidence for both theories, although the Uppsala model is the older of the two and may have been overtaken by events. The theories are not, of course, mutually exclusive.

The Internet, of course, means that any firm with a website is effectively trading globally, although many of these firms seem to be unaware of it. The result of all this internationalisation is that some marketing academics do not believe that international marketing should be taught as a separate subject at all – we are all international marketers now!

The key issues in international marketing include:

1 Should the firm standardise its marketing mix worldwide, or should it adapt to each local market?

2 How should the firm meet competition coming in from other countries?

3 How can the firm meet cultural differences in dealing overseas?

4 Which market entry methods are most appropriate?

5 Country-of-origin effects.

6 Global segmentation.

7 Psychological proximity.

You are likely to be asked questions on any of these topics, but more importantly the answers to these questions are likely to be relevant to most questions on international marketing.

The standardise/adapt debate depends in part on whether consumers in the target country will respond positively in terms of country of origin. This is about **customer perception** issues. In some cases, it is the very origin that makes the product acceptable – McDonald's has succeeded by being as American as it can be. Standardising improves economies of scale, but adaptation is likely to improve customer acceptance. You should bear in mind that products can be adapted without changing the brands or promotions, and vice-versa. Other parts of the marketing mix can be differentiated, too – prices are commonly different for the same product between different countries. Differential pricing is being made more difficult by two things: increased foreign travel, and the Internet. People can easily compare prices, and even shop abroad (as millions of British people do, crossing the Channel to shop in France. It is even easier for Northern Irish to buy their petrol in the Republic of Ireland).

> Note that it is the foreign consumer who decides whether the product is typical of its country of origin. What foreigners regard as typically British is a long way removed from what Britons regard as typically British (and the same is true of typically French, typically American, typically Japanese and so forth).

Meeting overseas competition can be difficult, because the foreign company has two advantages: first, it can afford to lose money in the foreign market because domestic sales will keep the company afloat until it becomes established. Second, it will (in the longer run) enjoy economies of scale. The domestic firm, of course, has the major advantages of knowing the market and already being established.

Culture is a major topic in international marketing. Obviously culture affects the product offering – products may need to be adapted considerably to meet local language, religious, or social conditions (McDonald's burgers are made of mutton in India, for instance). However, culture also affects the management of the firm (should managers be sent from the home country to manage the foreign workforce, or should local managers be recruited and risk the loss of a cohesive corporate culture), and relationships between the firm and its distributors. This is about **managing exchange**.

Culture also includes ways of doing business. This is often overlooked.

There are many ways of entering overseas markets, with varying degrees of risk and commitment attached. At the low end in terms of commitment, exporting via an agent involves minimal capital and minimal commitment, but carries long-term risks of losing control of what is happening in the foreign market. At the high end in terms of commitment, establishing a full overseas subsidiary is the biggest financial commitment, but also gives the most control over subsequent events. In general, smaller firms would be better to use the first approach, larger firms the second approach, but there are many variations in between.

Franchising or licensing works if one or more of the following conditions are satisfied:

1 The product does not travel well.

2 The firm has few resources for establishing itself abroad.

3 The product has good intellectual property protection, either through patent or copyright, or through strong branding.

4 The company and/or the product need strong local management.

Country-of-origin effect means that many companies and products are judged on the basis of the country they come from. Thus, Germans have a reputation for good engineering, Italians have a reputation for stylish design and so forth. There is only limited basis in fact for these assumptions: no doubt German universities do produce good engineers, but the most stylish German products are a great deal more stylish than the least stylish Italian ones, and the corresponding relationship would be true of engineering.

Global segmentation is about finding groups of people with similar needs, while ignoring national borders. As tastes converge worldwide, there will be more of these groups.

> *Remember that a segment in one country of, say, 56 million might be too small to be worth bothering with, but the same segment drawn from the world population of 6 billion would be over 100 times bigger!*

Psychological proximity is about doing business with countries that seem close because their culture is similar to that of the home country. For instance, many UK businesses happily enter the United States markets rather than the much more convenient French market, simply because they perceive Americans as being similar to Britons. In fact this is a dangerous assumption: as many Americans are of German or Latin descent as of British descent, and American culture is coloured by this. Also, American technical standards are different from UK standards – most EU technical standards have been standardised, with more being agreed every day.

> *Culture is only one issue among many in international business. You need to consider all aspects!*

The Internet is making a major difference to world markets, because it is impossible to differentiate the marketing mix on a website: even translating the site into different languages doesn't help, because many people understand other languages and in any case the numerals remain the same!

Taking it *FURTHER*

The debate on the benefits (or otherwise) of globalisation goes beyond the business community. There is a growing view that global trade will simply concentrate more wealth in the hands of already-wealthy nations. Added to this, there is the erosion of national cultures and diversity – when Starbucks target a city, they seek to out-compete all other coffee shops, so that the traditional kafenion in Greece, the cafés of Paris, the tea-rooms of rural England, and the café-bars of Spain are all potentially threatened.

The arrival of post-industrialism in Europe and the USA means that relatively little is made in those countries any more. Most manufacture is carried out in low-cost countries in the developing world: this probably means that the Uppsala model is obsolete, and Dunning's Eclectic Theory may not be far behind. The choices for market entry may be becoming fewer: exporting is laughable when everywhere else can make things cheaper, and expecting a foreign agent to compete with a major global corporation is also expecting rather a lot.

You may have already realised that the basic principles of marketing apply as much in overseas markets as they do in domestic markets, with the difference being that the foreign markets are much bigger. A recurring theme in international marketing is the effect of culture – so it is likely that an exam question will involve some consideration of cultural differences.

Remember that foreigners act differently, speak differently, think differently, buy different things, understand advertising in different ways, and like different things. This is what makes them foreign. However, the same is true of all individuals.

Here are some sample exam questions.

"Assume you are advising a British fast-food company planning on entering the French market. What factors might be important in deciding whether to adapt the marketing mix?"

Clearly the major factor will be cultural difference. The French are not generally as receptive to fast food as British people, and there will be a country of origin effect as well. The firm will obviously need to carry out research if the marketing mix is to be changed, but provided French people can accept that British food is edible and can even be desirable there will be no need to adapt the marketing mix, beyond translating everything into French.

In answering this question, you have the opportunity to discuss differentiated marketing in international markets, and also segmentation. There will be French people who have enjoyed British food, and also ex-pat Britons.

" Compare and contrast the Uppsala market-entry model with Dunning's Eclectic Theory. "

This question is straightforward in that you only need to know and understand the two competing theories. You will gain marks if you can demonstrate that the Uppsala model does not account for Internet marketing, and it is worth mentioning that the two theories are not mutually exclusive: some firms may follow the Uppsala route, others may follow some other route (which would match up with Dunning).

Textbook guide

ADCOCK, HALBORG AND ROSS: *Chapter 25.*
JOBBER: *Chapter 22.*
BRASSINGTON AND PETTITT: *Chapter 23.*
KOTLER, ARMSTRONG, SAUNDERS AND WONG: *Chapters 2 and 5.*
BLYTHE (2006): *Chapter 9.*

10

marketing strategy

Strategy is about doing the right things: tactics is about doing things right. Strategy is about where the firm is going: tactics is about how to get there.

The intention of marketing strategy is to place the company in the appropriate position relative to competitors and thus to gain competitive advantage: it therefore relates strongly to positioning (in the mind of the consumer) because marketing is **customer-centred**.

Textbooks and lecturers may teach strategy early in the course (to provide a framework for what is to come) or late in the course (as a way of bringing everything together). Many textbooks compromise by touching on the issues early, then filling in the detail towards the end of the book.

Creating competitive advantage is the basis of all business strategy: the marketing strategy may or may not be the same as the corporate strategy, depending on the degree to which the company is marketing orientated.

Michael Porter (1980) is the key thinker on strategy. He suggests that there are three winning strategies and one losing strategy, as follows:

1 *Overall cost leadership:* only one company in the market can have the lowest costs of production and distribution: this company will offer the cheapest products.

2 *Differentiation:* the company seeks to serve a number of market segments, each with a different product, and aims to become the industry leader.

3 *Focus:* the company concentrates on one or two niche markets, often markets which the industry leader does not think are worthwhile.

4 *Middle-of-the-road:* this is the failing strategy, an attempt to follow more than one of the above strategies will result in failure, or at least a less-than-optimum performance.

Tactics for each of these strategies differ. Market leaders stand to gain most from expanding the total market, and perhaps by increasing share still further. Market challengers set out to attack the market leader, either directly or by guerrilla tactics (picking off segments which are not well-served by the leader). Market followers do not challenge the leader (because a direct attack might breed retaliation). Market-nichers choose a specialist market and excel in it, under the noses of the leaders.

> *Most of the terminology in strategy comes from warfare. This is the key to understanding the thought processes of strategists.*

A recent development is **hypercompetition,** which is competition that breaks all the rules. In a hypercompetitive environment, firms deliberately try to disrupt the market, using hit-and-run tactics to disorientate the leaders and throw long-term plans out of order.

Strategic planning begins with one of two elements:

1 *A mission statement:* this is a statement about the purpose of the organisation. It will state what business the company is in, who the customers are, what the firm is in business for, and what sort of business we are.

2 *A vision statement:* this is about the values of the organisation, the corporate culture, or the 'personality' of the organisation.

Mission statements and vision statements are not mutually exclusive.

Planning continues with a decision about target markets: which markets should the company be in, in order to achieve the mission and conform with the vision? The next stage is to consider which competitors will be encountered in the markets, and how the firm will develop competitive advantage. This will lead to marketing mix decisions, which will then need to be implemented, and finally a control and evaluation system needs to be in place to ensure that targets are met and the strategy is effective.

There are six elements for testing the core strategy:

1 A successful strategy defines target customers and their needs. This is relevant to **customer centrality**.

2 The strategy should create a competitive advantage.

3 It should incur acceptable risk.

4 It should be supportable in terms of resources and management.

5 It should achieve product/market objectives.

6 It should be internally consistent.

Most strategy actually happens on an ad hoc basis. Most managers inherit an existing strategy, mission, vision, and so forth and only tinker with it.

Strategic objectives can be broken down for each product. The four basic product strategies are:

1 Build.
2 Hold.

3 Harvest.
4 Divest.

These strategies will be appropriate for different products according to lifecycle stage, product portfolio management, and overall corporate objectives. There is more on this in Section 12, Managing products.

You may be asked to formulate a marketing strategy or analyse an existing strategy. You will certainly be asked to do this if you are studying for the CIM Diploma, which has a case study approach to strategy. This being so, you will need to consider the strategy in the light of the above six items.

Control systems should be designed with the following in mind:

1 Feedback should not be about getting back on course: it should be about setting a new course to take us from where we are now to where we want to be.

2 Control systems theory is based on engineering: feedback of deviations and subsequent control behaviour may not work for people.

3 Control and feedback need to be set at appropriate levels and frequency for the industry. Rapidly changing industries need more frequent feedback.

Taking it **FURTHER**

The Porter model of competitive positioning is widely taught, but is sometimes considered to be over-simplistic. For example, it does not explain how low-cost airlines can all be aiming to be lowest-cost provider: at the same time, each one is differentiating itself by offering different routes from the others. This is not, however, a middle-of-the-road strategy.

In fact, all companies differentiate their products somewhat from their competitors – even oil companies try to differentiate their petrol, which is a fairly difficult thing to do since it is all identical, and has to be for cars to run on it.

Low-cost airlines also pose another problem: should they consider themselves to be offering only one product (air transport) or should they consider each route as a separate product? Much depends on whether the routes can be considered to be competing with other low-cost carriers. Some routes are obviously directly competing – both Ryanair and EasyJet fly from Stansted to Almería, for example. Other routes may compete in some ways: EasyJet flies to Malaga from Bristol, while BMI Baby flies to Malaga from Cardiff, about 40 miles away. For some customers, Cardiff is as easy to get to as Bristol and therefore the routes compete directly, while for people living in Cardiff the BMI Baby flight is much easier to use.

These issues are poorly explained by the model: like all models it is a simplification of the real world, intended to help understand a phenomenon and think about it more clearly.

Exam questions may revolve around the differences between corporate strategy and marketing strategy, or may examine details in the development of strategy. Here is an example:

"What competitive strategy option might be open for a small manufacturer of sports cars? What risks might such a company incur?"

A small manufacturer would have a very limited product range – probably only one or two models. Against the major producers (who follow a differentiated strategy) a small company would need to follow a focus strategy. The main risk would be that a major might seek to enter the same market, or that (having all its eggs in a very small basket) the company might fail to please its customer base sufficiently with its one or two products.

Another example might be:

"What is the difference between a mission statement and a vision statement? How do these statements affect the development of strategy?"

A mission statement is about where the company is going. A vision statement is about what the company is. The main difference in practice is that a mission can be achieved, which of course leaves the company with a problem in developing a new mission. A vision is simply a statement about what kind of company the firm is, and how it relates to its stakeholders: even if this is achieved, it will not need to be revised.

In terms of developing strategy, a mission statement provides much of the strategic direction already, whereas a vision asks questions rather than provides answers.

Textbook guide

ADCOCK, HALBORG AND ROSS: *Chapters 5 and 21.*
JOBBER: *Chapters 2 and 20.*
BRASSINGTON AND PETTITT: *Chapter 20.*
KOTLER, ARMSTRONG, SAUNDERS AND WONG: *Chapters 3 and 12.*
BLYTHE (2006): *Chapter 10, Chapter 12.*

11	
relationship marketing	

Relationship marketing was the buzz word of the 1990s and it still commands a great deal of interest among marketers. The conceptual basis for it is simple: it is cheaper to keep an existing customer than it is to recruit a new one. Andrew Ehrenberg summed this up neatly by comparing most firms' marketing to a leaky bucket – the marketers keep topping up the stock of customers, ignoring the customers who are leaking out of the bottom of the bucket. Relationship marketing seeks to plug the leaks.

The concept goes further – it is also cheaper to re-enlist a customer who has defected to a competitor than it is to recruit someone who is totally unfamiliar with the firm and its products. This is about helping customers **reach their objectives**.

Relationship marketing has the following key concepts:

1 It is cheaper to keep a customer than to recruit one.

2 Customers should be judged on their lifetime value, not on a single transaction.

3 Small changes in retention rates have very large effects on future revenues.

4 Building loyalty is the key to developing the relationship.

5 Building the relationship means both parties need to be adaptable.

Relationship marketing has been much more successful in B2B environments than in B2C, where most of the advantages are on the side of the firm and consumers do not usually feel that they will benefit from having a deeper relationship – this is a deviation from **customer centrality**. This is why relationship marketing is usually dealt with under business-to-business marketing.

The key thinker in relationship marketing was Theodore Levitt, who outlined the courtship-and-marriage analogy (Levitt, 1983). Business relationships are thought to go through similar stages: initial contact and attraction, followed by increasing contact and a desire to please the other party, ending with a long-term daily involvement and a shared life. There is, of course, the possibility of a painful and usually disruptive divorce later.

This model has been criticised (notably by Caroline Tynan) for being over-simplistic and not considering the possibilities of one-night stands, seduction, and even rape (where the power discrepancy between the firms is too great). It is worthwhile familiarising yourself with these arguments, because it enables you to demonstrate a degree of criticality. You might also consider whether Caroline Tynan is right, of course!

Relationships go through distinct stages, as follows:

1 *Pre-relationship stage:* the customer is evaluating a new supplier, perhaps because of dissatisfaction with an existing supplier.

2 *Early stage:* first orders are being placed, usually as a test to evaluate the supplier.

3 *Development stage:* purchase levels increase, and the firms' buyers and salespeople develop a closer working relationship. The firms begin to adapt their systems and procedures so that they work better together. This is customer centrality in action.

4 *Long-term stage:* the firms work closely together at all levels: new products are developed jointly, administrators work together to harmonise procedures, and so forth.

5 *The final stage:* the dealings between the firms have become institutionalised, so that any deviation from the usual pattern is likely to be met with opposition.

> *The key element in relationship marketing is building trust.*

The effects of taking a relationship marketing approach are likely to be as follows:

1 Firms will have fewer suppliers.

2 There will be mutual investment in the relationship in terms of adaptation and commitment.

3 Partnership will be the paradigm rather than negotiation.

4 Communication will be frequent between the firms at all levels.

5 Operations will become integrated.

6 Emphasis will be on lowest overall cost for both firms, rather than on lowest price from the supplier.

Many B2C firms still try to establish relationships with their customers, with greater or lesser success rates. Much of the relationship building is carried out proactively by the firm, however, using direct mail, e-mail, SMS texting or telemarketing: few consumers can see much benefit in establishing long-term relationships except with their banks, and even then they do not want regular telephone calls or mail in most cases.

 Taking it **FURTHER**

First, one of the danger areas with relationship marketing is that firms become too dependent on the few other firms with which they have a relationship, and get into trouble if the relationship ends. Second, in B2C markets relationship marketing's emphasis on lifetime value has led (for example) to an over-emphasis on recruiting young consumers, ignoring older consumers who actually have more money and more time to spend it, and are more likely to become loyal anyway. Third, power relationships are such that it is likely to be the supplying firm that does most of the adapting: hence Caroline Tynan's critique of the marriage analogy.

Finally, the picture is too simplistic. Firms (and consumers for that matter) have many relationships with many firms, which means that they would need to make many adaptations in their behaviour to meet the criteria of all the firms. A simple example is the widespread insistence by firms on customers using passwords to access the 'members only' areas of websites. Since the firms all have different systems for the passwords (some are numerical, some are letters, some combine the two, some are case-sensitive, and so on) customers find themselves with long lists of passwords to remember, or (conversely) having to write them down somewhere, allowing any passing burglar to access their bank accounts, stockbrokers, insurance companies, frequent-flyer accounts, and so forth.

Exam questions on relationship marketing are likely to consider the long-term benefits rather than the short-term problems. Here are two sample questions:

"What are the main differences between relationship marketing and transaction marketing? What are the benefits to the customer in establishing a relationship with a supplier?"

The differences are straightforward: transaction (traditional) marketing focuses on the immediate sale; relationship marketing focuses on the long-term income stream. You will need to provide a detailed list of the differences, but since different texts and lecturers give slightly different lists, you should go with the one you have been taught.

The benefits to the customer are: less time spent negotiating, more reliable supply, lower transaction costs, better quality control, and more efficient new-product development.

"What are the potential problems in adopting a relationship marketing approach to consumer markets?"

The main difficulty is that consumers often do not want to have a close relationship with the companies whose goods they buy. Many of them prefer to shop around, and actually resent being contacted by companies which they have bought from in the past.

A further problem is that relationship marketing looks at the lifetime value of a customer, and human beings age. This may lead to an over-emphasis on younger customers at the expense of ignoring older customers, who are actually much wealthier and have more time to spend on enjoying themselves.

Textbook guide

ADCOCK, HALBORG AND ROSS: *Chapters 7 and 12.*
JOBBER: *Chapter 4.*
BRASSINGTON AND PETTITT: *Chapter 4.*
KOTLER, ARMSTRONG, SAUNDERS AND WONG: *Chapter 11.*
BLYTHE (2006): *Chapters 11 and 17.*

12	
managing products	

A product is defined as a bundle of benefits. This is of course a consumer's view of the product: it is not a set of features, it is what it will do for the person. **Customer centrality** is the running theme. This way of looking at products leads to certain logical conclusions:

1 There is little conceptual difference between a service and a physical product: each might give similar benefits, and ultimately a physical product is only purchased because it provides intangible benefits.

2 Firms might be competing against other firms which appear to be in a different industry.

Marketing lecturers commonly talk about 'the product' as if the company only has one product. In fact, most companies have a wide range of products, a product portfolio. In order to ensure that the firm continues to satisfy customer needs efficiently, marketers need to manage this portfolio, adding new products as necessary and removing products which are no longer viable.

Products can be organised into product lines: groups of products with similar characteristics. Astute marketers will organise the products along consumer-orientated lines rather than product features.

A product consists of the core product (the basic features that would be expected of any product in the category), the tangible product (the features that are added to distinguish the product from its competitors), and the augmented product (which includes the intangibles such as the brand values and the service element).

If you always consider a product in terms of how it will improve people's lives you will not go far wrong.

Products can be classified in several different ways. Some writers and lecturers use a product-based classification (durable products, non-durable products, service products), while others prefer a consumer based classification system (convenience goods, shopping goods, speciality goods, and unsought goods). Each classification system has merits, depending on the situation.

The classification of products as being either physical products or service products is somewhat artificial: almost all physical products carry with them a service element, and almost all service products carry a physical element. From a consumer viewpoint, either one might provide similar benefits (a night out at a restaurant or a new outfit might both provide a much-needed morale boost, for example).

Products are assumed to go through a lifecycle (the **PLC**): they move from the introductory phase, when sales and profits are low, through a growth stage during which sales increase and profits begin to come in, to a maturity phase where sales and profits peak out, and eventually into a decline phase when the product is becoming obsolete.

> *The PLC is useful in understanding that products will lose money at first, will make money in their middle life, and eventually be superseded by newer and better products. It is not, however, a predictive tool because it is not possible to say how long each phase will last.*

Key issues in product portfolio management are as follows:

1. The product lifecycle tells us that all products eventually become obsolete and disappear. In other words, they cease to be effective in **helping customers meet their objectives**.

2. Products in the portfolio might be stars (having a high share of a growing market), cash cows (with a high share of a mature market), question marks (a small share of a growing market) or dogs (a small share of a mature market).

3. Products might be maintained in the portfolio if they have strategic significance.

4. Marketers need to have a new product development strategy in place if they are to be able to replace products which are dropped from the portfolio.

Planning for new products is essential if the firm is not to end up only with obsolete products. Looked at from a consumer's viewpoint, there are four categories of new product:

1 **Product replacement:** these account for about 45 per cent of new products, and are improvements or new models of existing products.

2 **Additions to existing lines:** about 25 per cent of new products, these are mainly brand extensions – variations on existing lines.

3 **New product lines:** about 20 per cent of launches, these represent a move into a new market.

4 **New-to-the-world products:** these represent about 10 per cent of new products, and are radically different products (for example DVD recorders, or mobile telephones).

Some lecturers and textbooks use a classification developed by Robertson (1967), which categorises innovations as continuous, dynamically continuous, or discontinuous. Continuous innovation follows on from previous products. Dynamically continuous innovations meet the same needs, but in a novel way. Discontinuous innovations meet new needs in a new way.

Another common way of looking at new products is from the producer's viewpoint. These categories are connected to producers' new product strategy.

1 **Innovative strategy:** some companies like to be first with a new idea: this gives first-to-market benefits, allowing the firm to become established before competitors bring out their own versions of the product. It is a high-risk, high-return strategy because most innovative products fail.

2 **Imitative strategy:** some companies prefer to let market leaders take the risk, then produce their own 'me-too' version of the product. This is a low-risk, low-return strategy: firms do not go bankrupt operating as imitators.

3 **Differentiation strategy:** rather than a straight me-too, the firm produces an improved product which meets the same needs as the original product.

4 **Niche strategy:** the company enters the market when it is mature, producing a version of the product which is aimed at a small segment (often one which is too small to interest the major firms).

5 **Late entry strategy:** these firms are likely to fail: other products are already well-established and the market is mature, so unless the firm actually buys an existing brand, it is unlikely to be able to succeed.

New product development is supposed to go through a series of stages. In practice, firms often omit stages, or the managing director gets a 'wonderful' idea which therefore is produced, despite the protests of the marketing department (the Sony Walkman is the commonest example given, but only because no one can think of another product which has succeeded by going this route. There are plenty of examples of spectacular failures – the Sinclair C5 is the commonest example of this).

Here are the stages:

1 New-product strategy.
2 Idea generation.
3 Screening.
4 Concept testing.

5 Business analysis.
6 Product development.
7 Market testing.
8 Commercialisation.

Developing an innovative corporate culture is a good idea for most firms: if innovation is discouraged (or even left unsupported) the company will quickly only have obsolete products left in the portfolio.

Some lecturers and textbooks include consumer innovative behaviour under new product development, others put it in with consumer behaviour. The most commonly-quoted model of adoption of innovation is that of Everett Rogers. Rogers (1983) categorised customers as follows:

1 *Innovators:* these are people who like to have the latest products. They are the first to buy: in many cases, this is about **meeting their objectives** of being 'firstest with the mostest'.

2 *Early adopters:* these people enter early, but like to let innovators take the risk of buying something which, after all, may not work.

3 *Early majority:* these people wait until the product is in use, and the bugs are out of the design.

4 *Late majority:* these people only buy when most people already have the product.

5 *Laggards:* these people are extremely reluctant to buy the product, and only do so when it is clear that there are few other options.

> Rogers' research was carried out among farmers, so it is based on a B2B market not a B2C market. This is a useful thing to bear in mind in an exam! Also, the cut-off points between the categories are based on statistical convenience, not on characteristics of the people involved – the reasoning is therefore circular.

Being an innovator for one category of product does not mean that the person is an innovator for a different category, of course. You may have noticed from the diagram of Rogers' classifications that it bears an unsurprising similarity to the product life cycle diagram. According to Gatignon and Robertson (1985), the following factors determine whether a product will be adopted or not:

1 Observability or communicability.
2 Trialibility, or divisibility.
3 Complexity.
4 Compatibility with existing lifestyle.
5 Relative advantage.
6 Perceived risk (social, financial, physical).

Taking it **FURTHER**

Much of the theory assumes a logical development of new products, and of adoptions by consumers. In fact, the rate of change in many markets means that many products have to be rushed through the process, and frequently people buy products without really thinking through the consequences of ownership.

The evolutionary view of innovation says that new products will succeed or fail by survival of the fittest – in other words, there is really no way of predicting what will succeed or fail, because too many new products are being launched at any one time, and no one can tell which of them might appear at the same time as our new product. Also, consumers are notoriously unpredictable – they are a lot like people in that respect.

In simple terms, levels of uncertainty are so high in new product development that it is virtually impossible for firms to predict what will happen.

Remember, when answering exam questions on innovation, it is innovation from the consumer's view that matters most to marketers. You are likely to be asked about Rogers' classification of adopters, or Robertson and

Gatignon's factors in adoption. Even if you are asked about the innovation process within the firm, you should not ignore the consumers!

Here are some sample questions.

" How might a company speed up the adoption process and thus shorten the growth stage of the PLC? "

This question requires you to show that you have an understanding of both the PLC and Rogers' adoption process model. You should answer the question by using Robertson and Gatignon's factors, something on the lines of:

The key to speeding the adoption process is to consider the needs of innovators, early adopters, and early majority. Innovators are likely to be most interested in observability and communicability, since their motivation is likely to be showing off the product to their friends and neighbours. Early adopters are more likely to be interested in relative advantage, so the aspects should be emphasised shortly after launch. Finally, early majority adopters are likely to be more interested in compatibility and complexity issues. If the company is interested in promoting to late majority and laggards, perceived risk is likely to be most important, but at this stage the product is probably fairly secure in its market.

" If most new products fail, why do companies innovate? "

The main reason that companies introduce new products is because the product lifecycle model shows us that, eventually, all new products will become obsolete and disappear. For an individual company, this would mean that the company would fail.

Another reason is that innovation helps to establish the company better in consumers' minds: 'new improved' is a good way of attracting attention.

For this question, you would also need to consider what the definition of failure is – it may be that a product has been a financial failure, but has opened up a strategic market.

Textbook guide

ADCOCK, HALBORG AND ROSS: *Chapter 11.*
JOBBER: *Chapters 9 and 10.*
BRASSINGTON AND PETTITT: *Chapters 7, 8 and 9.*
KOTLER, ARMSTRONG, SAUNDERS AND WONG: *Chapters 13 and 14.*
BLYTHE (2006): *Chapters 12 and 13.*

13	
pricing	

Price is often taught as being the only aspect of the marketing mix that generates income. There is an element of truth in this, but actually price goes a lot further than this: it is also part of the promotion mix, and helps in establishing brand values.

Price is what the customer has to pay for the product. In most cases, this is only considered in terms of what the marketer is paid for the product, but it is worth remembering that this is only part of the overall cost to the customer. There will be future running costs, and associated costs such as adapting one's lifestyle to fit around the product. These are called switching costs, because they relate to the costs of switching from an existing solution to a new (presumably better) solution.

Economists take the view that people will always seek to pay the lowest possible price for products, all things being equal. This may be true if all things were equal, but of course they are not: and in any case, there are too many examples where people prefer to pay more for what is substantially the same product, simply for prestige reasons. For example, a man taking his wife out for an anniversary dinner might order Vienna steak and French fries, and drink Perrier: what he actually has is a hamburger and chips with a glass of water, but he would not take his wife to a chip shop or hamburger restaurant for an anniversary dinner (not if he wants to see another anniversary, anyway). The anniversary dinner will not be as cheap, but it will represent value for money in the eyes of the man paying for it, because he is prepared to pay extra for the surroundings, the service, and of course the pleasure of looking good in the eyes of his wife! Value for money is the relationship between what you got and what you paid: what you got is a subjective judgement, so **consumer perceptions** of value for money differ between different people.

Remember that people do not always (or indeed often) buy the cheapest, but they always do buy what represents value for money.

There are various pricing methods in use, as follows:

1 *Cost-plus pricing:* this is taught on accountancy courses. The total costs of producing the product are totalled up, and a profit margin is added on. It is not really appropriate for marketers, because it ignores the customer entirely, but it is sometimes used in a few specialist markets. A variation, mark-up pricing, is used by retailers: they simply mark up the price by a fixed percentage on the price they paid for the goods themselves.

2 *Demand pricing:* the product is priced at a level which matches demand with the optimum level of production for the company. If pricing this way does not allow the company to make a profit, the product should be dropped (unless there is a strategic reason for keeping it in the portfolio).

3 *Psychological pricing:* this is pricing to position the product in the **consumer's** mind: high price often equates to high quality in most people's **perceptions**, low price often equates to thrifty management of money. Psychological pricing also includes **odd-even pricing** (99p endings on prices).

4 *Competition-based pricing:* the company seeks to position itself relative to competitors by its pricing. This does not necessarily mean pricing below the competition – the company might be seeking an upmarket position.

Competing on price is the last refuge of the incompetent, because it implies cutting profits. It's much better to compete by differentiating the product or promotion.

Pricing is often used as a part of sales promotion. Temporary discounts are offered in order to increase sales in the short term. There is more on sales promotion later in the book.

In an ideal world, marketers would only concern themselves with consumers' perceptions of price and value for money. Unfortunately, the costs of producing the product do need to be taken into account (if only to make a go/no-go decision). Costs divide into fixed costs (costs which do not vary with the quantity of product sold, for example factory overheads and tooling-up costs), variable costs (which increase or decrease according to the quantity produced, for example raw materials and components) and marginal costs (the change that occurs in the total cost if one more item is made). For the organisation, the difference between the cost of producing the product and the revenue from selling it is the contribution to overall profit.

Break-even point is the number of units which would need to be sold for the costs of production to equal the revenues earned. This is a useful figure to calculate, because it tells the planners at what point the product should become profitable. A slight difficulty with calculating break-even is that the company may find that it needs to offer discounts or increase its marketing budget in order to sell the required number – in which case the costs will rise and the calculations will need to be revised.

In international markets, demand-based pricing becomes problematic because of local economic conditions across a range of markets. What seems like value for money in a wealthy European country might seem impossibly expensive in a country such as Indonesia or Thailand. Because the marginal cost of producing a few more items for sale in these countries might be small, the firm might be able to afford to sell at a lower price in those countries and still make a profit overall. This is called **second-market discounting**, or sometimes **differential pricing**. It is about **helping customers reach their objectives**.

Offering the same product for different prices in different markets makes sense for the marketer, but may not make sense to a consumer: people often travel to other countries to take advantage of lower prices (at the time of writing, it was worthwhile for people to fly from the UK to the USA in order to buy computer equipment).

Differential pricing (second-market discounting) has become much more difficult since the Internet gave people access to overseas distributors and their websites.

Second-market discounting has led to the re-importation of some products. US textbooks call this the **grey market,** but in the UK the grey market also refers to marketing to people over 50 (beware of terminology if you are set an assignment on the grey market!) A landmark legal case in the UK (between Tesco and Levi Strauss) established the manufacturer's right to prevent re-importation of goods.

Sometimes it is the buyer who sets the price. Internet auctions are an example in B2C marketing; tendering is an example in B2B marketing.

In tendering situations, buyers present a detailed specification and invite bids – usually the lowest bidder gets the job. There are three approaches to survival in a tender situation:

1 Talk to the buyer before the tender is drawn up and ensure that something is entered which the competition cannot meet.

2 Ensure that the contract contains large extra payments for any deviation from the original specification. On any large project, there will be deviations, and it is here that the company will make its profit.

3 Collude with other suppliers to arrange who will win the bid. This is not only unethical, it is also illegal in most countries.

Taking it **FURTHER**

Marketers often advise companies to avoid competing on price, but instead to offer more features, more variety or better service. This makes some kind of sense – if the cost of providing the extras is lower than the extra premium the firm can charge, then both the consumer and the company will be better off. However, there are several examples of cases where this strategy has gone horribly wrong – for instance, in the USA all the car manufacturers were offering ever-bigger, ever-faster, ever-better equipped cars. This allowed Japanese manufacturers to enter the market with smaller, cheaper, more basic models.

Competing on price is fine if there are no other companies in the market with the same idea – if everyone tries to undercut everyone else, the result is a price war which will be won by the firm with the deepest pockets – and which will then raise prices to recoup its losses.

Pricing is a great deal less straightforward than would at first appear, because it affects almost everything else the company does.

There is not much theoretical basis to pricing, so most exam questions are likely to concentrate on practical aspects. You may be asked to calculate prices (one of the few areas in marketing where you will need a calculator), but your lecturer would probably give you plenty of advance hints if this is the case. Otherwise, you are likely to be asked to compare different pricing methods or give the advantages and disadvantages of each approach.

Here are two examples.

"What are the disadvantages of cost-plus pricing? Why would a retailer use mark-up pricing rather than demand pricing?"

In this question, you are being asked to criticise cost-plus pricing, and then justify its near relative, mark-up pricing. This requires some mental gymnastics! The disadvantage of cost-plus is that it ignores the customer; the advantage is that it is quick and simple. For the retailer, something quick and simple is necessary because of the sheer number of products on offer, and retailers are close enough to the customer to be able to reduce the price if the product fails to sell – it can always go into the January sales!

Remember also that pricing is not only about managing exchange, it is also about perceptions.

"How does pricing interrelate with promotion?"

Pricing interrelates with promotion in two directions: promotion often mentions price, and prices are often adjusted (usually downwards) as a sales promotional tool.

For extra marks, it is worth mentioning that promotion is about sending out appropriate signals, and prices offer signals about quality and value for money. In a sense, therefore, pricing is itself a promotional tool in a direct way.

Textbook guide

ADCOCK, HALBORG AND ROSS: *Chapter 14.*
JOBBER: *Chapter 11.*
BRASSINGTON AND PETTITT: *Chapters 10 and 11.*
KOTLER, ARMSTRONG, SAUNDERS AND WONG: *Chapters 16 and 17.*
BLYTHE (2006): *Chapter 14.*

14	
advertising	

Advertising is the paid insertion of a message in a mass medium. It is a part of publicity; it is not the whole of it. Non-marketers often use phrases such as 'free advertising', which does not fit the definition – what they mean is 'free publicity', which is different.

It is worthwhile being careful about your terminology – this shows that you know how to think like a marketer.

Advertising might be about promoting products, or it might be about improving the corporate image, or it may have elements of both. Advertising can be presented through a number of mass media: essentially, it is an impersonal type of communication, so targeting is usually somewhat hit-and-miss. The exception is when advertising is targeted through very specific media such as specialist magazines, but even then most advertising expenditure is wasted because the message goes to the wrong people.

Categories of advertising are as follows:

1 **Pioneering advertising:** this is advertising intended to launch a new product and explain its benefits to people who did not previously know it existed.

2 **Competitive advertising:** this differentiates the product from its competitors.

3 **Comparative advertising:** this draws direct comparison between the firm's products and those of its competitors. It needs to be used with care – sometimes people develop sympathy for the company under attack, especially if they have just bought that company's product. Also, comparative advertising publicises the competitor's name: people often forget the comparison but remember the brand!

4 **Reminder advertising:** the intention here is to remind customers of the product's existence. This is used for established products, to ensure that competitors do not move in.

5 *Institutional advertising:* this promotes the company rather than the brands.

Planning advertising follows this formula:

1	Decide the target audience.	5	Develop the advertisement.
2	Decide the advertising platform.	6	Buy space.
3	Formulate the message.	7	Run the advertisement.
4	Decide on the medium.	8	Assess the results.

There are various platforms for advertising: fear avoidance, saving money, enhancing security, and so forth. The actual message involves a creative input – it is not susceptible to advice, except that it is usually better to do something different from what the competition are doing. You are unlikely to be asked to design an advertisement in an exam, but you might be set this as an assignment task, depending on which course you are taking.

Choice of medium depends on budget, what the message is and what the product is as well as on the fit between advertising and the rest of the marketing effort. Press advertising has the advantage that it is permanent – people can cut out the advertisement, or write down telephone numbers or addresses from it. TV and cinema have the advantage that the image is moving, and there is sound, so it engages more of the individual's senses (note that cinema has a captive audience, which TV certainly does not have). Radio has the advantage of being cheap, of having a captive audience, and of offering an active presentation through sound.

Ambient advertising is a relative newcomer. Ambient advertisements are part of the environment – slogans on stair risers, advertisements on the back of bus and train tickets, slogans on petrol-pump nozzles, in fact advertising anywhere where it is difficult for the audience to ignore.

Outdoor advertising (billboards, transport advertising, and so on) has the advantage of being cheap and having a high impact in the areas in which it appears. Transport advertising has the unique feature that it can take a lot of copy – all other advertising requires extremely brief copy, because people will not take time to read it. On buses and trains, people have little else to do but read the ads!

Choosing a medium may involve some careful calculation. Typically, marketers look at reach, frequency and ratings. Reach is the number of the target audience that might reasonably be expected to see the advertisement at least once during the relevant period. Frequency is the average number of times the target audience will have been exposed to the advertisement during the relevant period. Rating is the number of people who would see the TV show in which the advertisement appears (the equivalent for press advertising is circulation or readership).

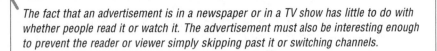

> *The fact that an advertisement is in a newspaper or in a TV show has little to do with whether people read it or watch it. The advertisement must also be interesting enough to prevent the reader or viewer simply skipping past it or switching channels.*

In most cases, marketers use an advertising agency. The advantage is that the agency is mainly paid by the media, in the form of commissions. Choice of agency should be according to the following criteria:

1 **The size of the agency should reflect the size of the client:** big agency, big client.

2 **Location and accessibility:** client and agent need to be able to talk regularly with each other.

3 **Type of help required:** a full-service agency will provide help with planning a campaign and designing advertisements as well as with booking media space.

4 **Specialism:** some agencies specialise in particular product categories or consumer groups.

5 **Track record:** how has the agency done in the past?

6 **Compatibility, empathy, personal chemistry:** can the client and the agency work well together?

7 **Business ability:** can the agency work within budget, and produce results on time?

> *You may be asked to outline an approach to assessing an advertising agency. Since this is more typical of what practitioners do (rather than producing advertisements themselves) you should be clear about the issues.*

Evaluating advertising is notoriously difficult, because most advertising operates below the conscious level. In other words, people have trouble remembering where they first heard of the company. The techniques commonly in use are:

1 ***Unaided recall:*** consumers are asked to remember which advertisements they can remember.

2 ***Aided recall:*** consumers are asked which advertisements from a given list they can remember.

3 ***Attitude tests:*** people are asked about their attitudes towards a product. This would usually be carried out with two representative samples of consumers – one group before the advertising campaign is run, the second group after it is run.

4 ***Enquiry tests:*** the number of requests for more information is logged before and after the campaign, to see if there is any difference.

5 ***Sales tests:*** sales levels are checked before and after the campaign. This is notoriously unreliable, because too many other factors might have affected sales.

Communications campaigns can only be measured in terms of communications outcomes, not by marketing outcomes.

 Taking it **FURTHER**

Some recent research has indicated that traditional methods of assessing television advertising are seriously ineffective. The current method is to use a monitoring system attached to the television sets of a large panel of volunteers. The equipment records which programmes are being watched, and panel members keep a record of who is in the room at any one time. The records are integrated so that the marketers can say with a fair degree of certainty how many people were exposed to each advertisement.

Unfortunately it transpires that the record is incomplete. The fact that someone is in the room certainly does not mean that they are actually watching the advertisement. Researchers placed cameras on the TV sets and watched what people actually do: some immediately pick up a book or magazine and read through the break; some strike up a conversation; some take up household tasks such as mending socks or paying bills; some use the remote control to flip between channels (largely a male activity, for some reason). On the plus side, some people play games with the advertisements – a surprising number of people play 'guess the product', or sing along with the jingles, and some people actually just sit and watch the advertisements.

For advertisers, none of this is good news. TV advertising is extremely expensive, and although advertisers know that some people skip the advertisements, leave the room, or cut the advertising out of recorded programmes, they had always felt secure in the belief that the people actually in the room were watching the advertisements.

Will this spell the end of TV advertising? Possibly: the medium is under threat anyway – too many channels chasing too few advertisers, apart from anything else. Add the competition from new media, and the fact that far fewer people watch the advertisements than was previously thought, might be enough to kill TV stone dead. Watch this space! (If you're still in the room.)

Exam questions on advertising might ask you about creative issues or media choices, but will almost always expect you to consider advertising as a part of an integrated campaign. For example:

"What would be the key issues in planning an advertising campaign for a new car?"

Apart from the planning sequence outlines above, you should include something on budgeting (see the earlier section on communications theories). You should also explain what other promotional methods you intend to put in place and how these will fit with the timing of the campaign. Showing how the different media can feed each other is also useful.

On media choices, here is another example:

"What are the advantages and disadvantages of using television advertising as opposed to press advertising?"

Television is an impermanent medium, and cannot contain detailed copy: newspapers, on the other hand, cannot have the same impact as TV because they are static.

On a more subtle level, newspapers and TV have differing legal restrictions on what can and cannot be shown – newspapers actually have considerably more leeway.

In this question, it would be worthwhile mentioning the issue of skipping past advertising by 'zipping' and 'zapping' on TV. If you are particularly keen, you might also point out that people often buy newspapers specifically for the advertising (classified ads, cinema ads, and so on) whereas very few people turn on the TV for the advertising.

Textbook guide

ADCOCK, HALBORG AND ROSS: *Chapter 16.*
JOBBER: *Chapter 12.*
BRASSINGTON AND PETTITT: *Chapter 15.*
KOTLER, ARMSTRONG, SAUNDERS AND WONG: *Chapter 19.*
BLYTHE (2006): *Chapter 15.*

15
pr and sponsorship

PR (public relations) is about making the world feel good about the company and its products. Different textbooks and lecturers give it varying prominence as a topic, partly because public relations professionals often regard it as being a non-marketing function.

Several definitions are in current use, but the commonest one in UK textbooks is that of the Institute of Public Relations (www.instituteforpr. com), which runs as follows:

> PR is the deliberate, planned and sustained effort to institute and maintain mutual understanding between an organisation and its publics.

The definition needs some explanation, especially in terms of defining what is meant by 'publics'. **Publics** are any group which affects, or is affected by, the organisation's activities. In the case of a large company, this probably means the entire population, but it is broken down into discrete groups. One way of dividing these is:

1 *Commercial publics:* suppliers, customers, joint venture partners, etc.

2 *Internal publics:* staff, trade unions, management.

3 *Financial publics:* banks, shareholders, the wider financial community.

4 *Authority publics:* government, local government, trade associations, regulatory bodies.

5 *Media publics:* news media, entertainment media.

6 *General publics:* local community, neighbours, opinion formers, leaders, lobbying groups, pressure groups, in fact almost anybody not covered by the other categories.

PR will not replace other communications media, but it can certainly help in marketing products as part of an integrated campaign. Marketing PR, as opposed to corporate PR, is aimed at improving public perception of brands. Corporate PR is about improving perceptions of the organisation itself.

Tools of PR are as follows:

1 *Press releases:* these are news stories about the organisation.

> *Press releases must be newsworthy. This means they must offer something out of the ordinary: they should not be thinly disguised advertisements. You may be asked to write a press release for an assignment or even in an exam – try to avoid using too many adjectives and superlatives.*

2 *Press conferences:* a press conference is a way of getting a group of journalists together to announce something newsworthy.

3 *Events:* running a newsworthy event can create publicity.

4 *Corporate advertising:* running an advertisement aimed at enhancing corporate reputation.

5 *Annual reports:* reports to shareholders, banks, and so on seek to present the most positive aspects of the company to its financial publics.

6 Internal newsletters, magazines, and so on. These maintain a positive corporate image for internal publics.

7 *Staff briefings:* occasionally, PR people might want to brief staff on new developments within the firm.

8 *Sponsorship:* this is a partnership between the firm and a person or event. The person or event receives funding or other help, in exchange for which the organisation receives publicity.

PR techniques (especially press releases) are much more credible than advertising and much less likely to be avoided by the target audience. The main drawback is that they are not as easily-controlled as advertising.

Sponsorship is becoming a major force in publicity. The following types of event might receive sponsorship:

1 *Sporting events:* these often receive television coverage, but even if they do not the audiences at the event are potentially large.

2 *Broadcast sponsorship:* this is relatively new in the UK. The sponsoring company links itself to the programme, receiving a 'plug' before and after the show, and in the advertising breaks. These are prime spots, better than the advertising spots during the breaks, because people are waiting for the programme to return and will watch the sponsor's message. There are very strict rules governing broadcast sponsorship.

3 *Arts sponsorship:* sponsorship of festivals, concerts and performing arts generally can put the company in a good position relative to its target audience.

4 *Cause-related sponsorship:* sponsoring a charity or charitable event can raise the company's profile, and show it as a caring organisation.

The key to successful sponsorship is to ensure that there is a clear link between the brand and the event being promoted.

Sponsorship will help develop brand values provided the values of the sponsored object are similar to those of the brand. In recent years firms have become reluctant to sponsor individuals because of the risk of the individual falling from grace in some way: for example, sponsoring an athlete who is subsequently caught taking performance-enhancing drugs would not be good PR.

As with other communications media, assessing sponsorship is important but not simple. Measurement techniques include:

1 *Media exposure measurement:* how many times did the event feature in the news media?

2 *Communication outcomes:* did the sponsorship raise the corporate profile, or change people's attitudes, or whatever the aim of the exercise was?

3 *Measure sales results:* this is conceptually problematic: it is unlikely that measuring sales results would give any indication of the success or otherwise of the exercise. There might be some feedback possible this way if the sponsorship were linked to a sales promotion, but even then the sales could have risen or fallen for any number of reasons unconnected with the promotion.

4 Feedback from participating groups.

Since the Europe-wide ban on tobacco sponsorship, many arts and charitable organisations have been feeling the pinch, and some sporting events have disappeared altogether. There are therefore plenty of opportunities for sponsorship by other firms.

> *When approached to provide sponsorship, or even when applying to a firm for sponsorship, the key question to consider is 'What's the pay-off for the firm?'*

Taking it ***FURTHER***

PR is sometimes seen as a 'quick fix' option for companies with image problems. It has also been associated with so-called 'spin doctoring', in which an acceptable face is put on unacceptable facts. PR does not have the answer to everything, however – often the organisation needs to put its house in order first, so that the publicity machine has something good to say about it.

> The need to be newsworthy can lead press officers into dangerous areas – creating news, exaggerating, saying things about the company that are untrue or inappropriate. Interestingly, the restrictions on truthfulness that control advertising do not apply to press releases – a further temptation to apply spin!

Exam questions on sponsorship are likely to ask you for lists of advantages, disadvantages, and criteria for sponsorship activities. You are also likely to be asked to show how to integrate sponsorship into the rest of the marketing mix. Here is an example:

" What considerations would you need to take into account when approached to provide sponsorship? How would you maximise the returns from sponsoring, say, a charitable appeal? "

You would need to begin by listing the advantages and disadvantages of sponsorship. Then discuss the need for the sponsored event to contribute to the firm's overall brand values. To maximise return, you would need to show how you would link the sponsorship to advertising – promoting the charitable appeal, but with the corporate name prominent – and to PR (issuing press releases to publicise the appeal). You could even link the appeal to a sales promotion, offering to contribute a fixed amount to the appeal for every unit of product sold.

Questions on public relations often take a practical approach, asking you to write a press release or plan a PR campaign. Otherwise you might be asked a 'comparison' type question, as follows:

" Explain how PR fits in with other elements of the communications mix. What advantages does PR have over advertising, and what are its drawbacks? "

The first half of the question is largely descriptive: PR is about developing goodwill rather than encouraging specific action, whereas advertising, personal selling and sales promotion all seek to cause a specific response in the audience. The second half of the question is the comparison: PR has the advantage that it is more likely to 'get through' to the audience because they are less able to avoid it, and in many cases it can provide more information than can an advertisement. On the other hand, PR activities are much less controllable than advertising.

Textbook guide

ADCOCK, HALBORG AND ROSS: *Chapter 18.*
JOBBER: *Chapter 16.*
BRASSINGTON AND PETTITT: *Chapter 19.*
KOTLER, ARMSTRONG, SAUNDERS AND WONG: *Chapter 19.*
BLYTHE: *Chapter 16.*

16	
selling and key-account management	

Personal selling is marketing brought to the individual level. Probably the most powerful marketing tool available, a salesperson sitting in front of a buyer and giving a personalised problem-solving advice session, is probably also (in terms of number of contacts made per pound spent) the most expensive.

Salespeople operate by asking questions about the buyers' situation in order to identify problems and offer solutions. The image of the salesperson as a fast-talking, persuasive individual with a wide range of high-pressure techniques for forcing people to buy is a long way from the truth: people are not stupid enough to fall for that kind of approach.

The Theodore Levitt statement to the effect that marketing's role is to make selling obsolete refers to the selling CONCEPT, not the modern practice of selling.

Salespeople fall into a number of categories: the list varies, according to which textbook and lecturer you have, but some categories are common to all. These are:

1 *Missionary salespeople:* these people talk to influencers and deciders, but not buyers. A typical example is medical salespeople, who seek to persuade doctors to prescribe drugs, but do not talk to the pharmacists who actually stock them.

2 *New-business sales people;* these people talk to buyers and deciders in order to bring in new business.

3 *Inside order-takers:* these people wait by the telephone for buyers to ring them, or in some cases are proactive in calling existing customers in order to bring in sales.

4 *Outside order-takers:* these people call on existing customers to take their orders. They do not open new accounts.

5 *Delivery salespeople:* these people deliver goods directly to the customer, and take orders for more goods. This is typical of snack and crisp sales to small corner shops.

6 *Technical salespeople:* essentially technicians, these people sell to other technical or professional people in cases where the products are highly-technical or complex.

The selling cycle is usually drawn as a circle, because salespeople will follow round the circle in a repetitive way. In fact, the sales cycle only refers to one customer: salespeople will have several sales cycles running at once. The sales cycle runs as follows:

1 Prospecting.
2 Preparation and planning.
3 Initiating contact.
4 Sales presentation.
5 Handle objections.
6 Negotiation.
7 Close the sale.
8 After-sales activities.

> *These activities are likely to run concurrently even with the same customer. Objection-handling will happen throughout the presentation, not just at the end, and in fact so will a lot of closing activities.*

Salespeople do not operate by talking: they operate by listening. Sales presentations usually begin with a set of questions designed to determine what the customer's problem is and consider possible solutions from the selling company's repertoire of products. Good salespeople will agree with the buyer what the buyer's needs are before beginning to outline a solution. The next stage is to outline a solution, only touching on those aspects of the product which are relevant to the customer. With any luck, the customer will raise objections (problems with the solution). This indicates that the customer is serious about buying. The salesperson should hear the customer out without interrupting, then explain how the problem can be overcome: it is a good idea to check that the customer agrees with the solution offered. At the end of the presentation, the salesperson should close the sale (ask for the order), and may use any one of several techniques to help the customer over the decision making hurdle.

> *Salespeople should be problem-solvers, concerned for the customer's needs. Trying to sell somebody something they don't need is annoying for the customer and a total waste of time for the salesperson.*

Having made the sale, the salesperson should call back when the order has been delivered, and should act as the customer's contact back to the company if there are any problems with the product or the company.

The above routine works well for small-account sales, where the salesperson is likely to be speaking directly to the decision-makers. In dealing with larger accounts, salespeople are unlikely to be in that position: the decisions might be made at Board level, or by people the salesperson will not meet. **Key-account** selling therefore has a set of specialist techniques, most of which are not covered in an introductory course: suffice it to say that salespeople need to raise the profile of the problem in the eyes of the buyer in order to justify being referred to a higher decision-maker, and also to raise the value of the solution. A key account can be defined as one which has some or all of the following characteristics:

1 It represents a substantial proportion of the firm's business.

2 It is of strategic importance to the firm in some way.

3 It requires one or both parties to change the way they do business.

Managing salespeople is a process of:

1 *Recruiting the right people:* there is no way of knowing who can sell and who cannot. Talent is far less important than motivation.

2 *Training:* teaching people to sell, teaching them about the company, teaching them about the product range. Some of this happens in classrooms, but most of it happens in the field.

3 *Motivation:* this is separate from remuneration – there is some disagreement among academics about whether commission payments are motivational or not. Most sales managers run competitions, games, bonus schemes and the like as motivational devices, which would be unnecessary if commission were enough. Motivation theorists include Herzberg, Vroom and Maslow: their theories are outlined briefly in Section 1 on the underpinnings of marketing.

4 *Remuneration:* most salespeople are paid a combination of salary and commission. This is their reward for doing the job, compensating them for the time they give the company. It may not have much to do with motivation (unless the commission doesn't get paid, of course).

5 *Supporting people through rejection:* most salespeople lose more sales than they get, which is demotivating: sales managers need to be able to prop them up again when things go wrong.

6 *Managing long-distance:* salespeople may be based anywhere in the country (or in the world) and may therefore not see the sales manager for weeks or months at a time. Sales managers therefore need to be able to keep in contact with the salespeople on a regular basis.

You are more likely to be asked questions about sales management than about sales techniques, but it is definitely worthwhile being prepared for questions about either.

Taking it *FURTHER*

Personal selling is almost always taught as part of the communications mix. This may not be appropriate: sales people have a much wider role than communicating, since they also aim to help customers solve their supply problems. This problem-solving aspect takes salespeople out of the communication mix, even though they do their jobs by managing communication.

If this is so, it is fairly obvious that marketers can easily be led astray by trying to use salespeople as communicators. Salespeople will not simply repeat the marketers' carefully-prepared message, because they need to solve problems, and will therefore tell the customers whatever is necessary to get the sale. There is therefore a set of circumstances which is ripe for conflict!

Here is a typical exam question.

"How might you encourage the salesforce to put extra effort into launching a new product? What dangers might you need to beware of in using your chosen approach?"

This question is about motivation and training. The salespeople will need training on the features and benefits of the new product, and will need some kind of extra motivational input. For example, you might run a sales competition with a prize for the salesperson who sells the most of the new product, but beware of demotivating people who come last in the competition.

You might also be asked about key-account management, especially as this topic moves to the forefront in coming years.

"Why should managers try to avoid encouraging key-account salespeople to increase their activity levels?"

This is a crucial aspect of managing key-account people. In small sales, encouraging salespeople to see more clients almost always improves sales: in key accounts it has the reverse effect, because salespeople will tend to rush the process and lose sales, and what is worse will tend to aim for smaller accounts which are easier to sell.

Textbook guide

17	
# direct and online marketing	

Probably the single most important development in marketing in recent years is the advent of the Internet. From its beginnings as a means of sharing information between academics and military forces, the Internet has become almost entirely marketing-driven. Funded by advertising, free websites offer information, misinformation and outright lies to surfers: other sites are dedicated to selling goods.

During the 1990s, many wild claims were made about the future of the Internet. Some marketers went so far as to say that the Internet would replace traditional retailers almost entirely. This has not happened, and is unlikely to do so, for the following reasons:

1 *Delivery times are not precise:* people cannot wait around at home all the time for delivery firms to bring goods to them.

2 *Information overload:* the amount of information on the Internet is simply too large for people to wade through. Going to a retail shop is simpler.

3 *Access to the technology:* only a tiny proportion of the world's population has access to the Internet, and even in wealthy countries people with private access are in a minority.

4 *Security concerns:* many Internet users are fearful of using credit cards online because of the possibility of hackers stealing the details and 'cloning' the card.

5 *Cost implications:* the initial investment to go online is fairly high – many consumers simply do not have the money to do it, while others think that the money is better spent elsewhere.

6 *The absence of tangibility:* being able to pick up (say) a book and browse the contents is an extremely important part of shopping, available to only a limited extent on the Internet. Shopping is a plea- sure in itself – not just a way of buying stuff.

7 *Convenience:* Buying online is not always as convenient as (say) stepping out to a shop during one's lunch break. Having to wait several days for the goods does not help!

The Internet can be considered as being a very marked improvement on mail-order: mail order has most of the same advantages as the Internet, but is less interactive. Mail order accounts for around 4 per cent of UK retail sales – so why would the Internet do better?

One of the key results of Internet marketing is disintermediation. This is the process of cutting out the middle man – so that the Internet allows people to deal directly with the supplier. Although in some cases this has resulted in major savings (it is one of the main cost-cutting effects for low-cost airlines), it does not always follow that savings will be made, because distributors perform necessary functions which have to be per- formed by somebody else.

Having said that, the Internet does have real advantages, such as:

1 *Lower transaction costs:* with much of the work of processing orders either automated or transferred to the customer, costs for the supplier are lower.

2 *Improved service quality:* transactions are rapid online, and provided the orders are fulfilled promptly, the process is much faster and pleasanter than mail order.

3 *Greater product variety:* online stores can carry a much greater inventory than a retailer can, and the customer's search process is much faster than would be the case in a bricks-and-mortar store.

4 *Product customization:* in many cases, the product can be tailored to the consumer (Dell do this online).

5 *Closeness to the customer:* internet-based retailers can keep detailed records of who buys what, and build up a picture of what the customer might like to buy based on previous purchases.

There are two problems with writing about Internet marketing: one is that the Internet itself is changing on an almost daily basis, and the other is that relatively little research has been carried out compared with other marketing topics. In other words, there is limited experience out there and the situation is changing too fast for it to be of much help.

Promotion on the Internet falls into the following categories:

1 *Presence websites:* These are websites which give a few details about the firm, and drive enquiries towards e-mail, telephone or postal contacts. These are becoming fewer, as more firms make their websites interactive.

2 *Interactive websites:* these allow visitors to explore the website in search of specific information, or even to place orders online.

3 *Banners:* these are advertisements placed on free websites: it is one of the ways these websites are funded.

4 *Pop-ups:* these are messages which appear, unbidden, on the screen while the Internet user is accessing a website. Many Internet users now have pop-up blocking software, so it is possible that these will die out eventually.

5 *Hyperlinks to other associated websites:* often website owners enter into agreements with each other to set up hyperlinks to each others' websites.

In B2B marketing, electronic commerce predates the Internet. Many large firms and retailers used a system called electronic data interchange, in which customers' and suppliers' computers shared information via dedicated network connections. For example, some retailers' computers would telephone suppliers' computers overnight and tell them what had been sold during the day, so that the suppliers could arrange for fresh stocks to be delivered the following morning. This system was in use in the early 1970s. Nowadays, Internet-based systems have largely taken over from EDI.

Direct marketing comprises any marketing initiative which goes direct from supplier to consumer, and is intended to generate a direct response. Various definitions are used: the American Direct Marketing Association definition is:

> An interactive system of marketing which uses one or more advertising media to effect a measurable response at any location.

This definition is probably far too broad. It does not say what direct marketing is not, for example.

Direct marketing has shown a huge rise in popularity in recent years, for the following reasons:

1 *Changing demographics and lifestyles:* less time for shopping means people are more open to the idea of direct shopping via the mail.

2 Increased customer confidence in supplier organisations.

3 Increased competition in traditional retailing.

4 *Media fragmentation:* more magazines, more TV stations, more commercial radio stations, and so forth mean it is harder to reach people via mass media.

5 *Increasing media and sales costs:* direct marketing is often cheaper, because less of the effort is wasted contacting people who would never be interested anyway.

6 *New distribution channels:* improvements in logistics management mean more rapid and reliable deliveries to consumers.

7 *Increasing computer power and lower data processing costs:* more firms are able to handle high rates of response from individuals.

Direct marketing uses the following techniques:

1 *Direct mail:* the key to success here is to have an accurate, relevant mailing list.

2 *Telemarketing or teleselling:* using the telephone to contact people. This is often regarded as extremely intrusive by many customers.

3 *Direct-response advertising:* this is advertising where the *call to action* includes a response vehicle – a coupon, a telephone number, a website, or an e-mail address. It can be particularly effective on TV.

4 *Mail-order catalogues:* formerly these were aimed at poorer people, but catalogues like *Next* have moved the medium up-market.

Note that many direct marketing techniques have become highly-regulated in recent years. The Mail Preference Service and Telephone Preference Service have allowed consumers to opt out of receiving unsolicited calls, and the Data Protection Act makes it harder for firms to exchange mailing lists with each other. These are key issues in the future of direct marketing.

 Taking it **FURTHER**

Consumers are steadily growing wise to direct mail tactics. Nowadays people are reluctant to give out personal details to any company, and if they do they frequently give out slightly different details to different companies so that they can track where their details are being sold. This sometimes means that the same person will receive several mailings from the same company, because the address details are slightly different in each case.

In the 1990s some observers (notably Professor Martin Evans) believed that combining databases would eventually enable firms to build up an extremely detailed picture of individuals, such that privacy would be severely compromised. The dire warnings were heeded, and legislation was passed which effectively prevents this from happening. Such is the fear and hostility attached to direct mail and telesales that further legislation is likely: in the USA people can already opt out of receiving calls, with heavy penalties for firms who violate the ban: around 40 per cent of Americans have asked to be taken off the telesales lists.

This leaves us with the question – how customer-centred is direct marketing? Are marketers really intending to annoy and frighten their potential customers?

Questions on direct marketing tend to revolve around techniques, since there is very little theoretical base for it. Here are two examples:

"How might you go about establishing an e-mail list for a low-cost airline?"

Low-cost airlines sell their tickets online, so it should be fairly easy to capture the e-mail addresses of former customers. To expand the list further, you might want to consider buying in lists from such firms as travel insurance companies, because they deal with frequent travellers. Finally, a list could be derived by running a direct-response campaign in the press or on TV, perhaps with a free flight as an incentive to send in details.

"What steps might you take to improve the effectiveness of a direct mail campaign?"

There are many issues here. First and foremost, the campaign should be tightly targeted, using a clean mailing list. Second, the offer should be clearly stated and the action needed on the part of the audience should also be clear – it should be made as easy as possible for people to respond. Third, follow-up activities such as repeat mailings or telephone calls are likely to increase response rates.

Textbook guide

ADCOCK, HALBORG AND ROSS: *Chapter 17.*
JOBBER: *Chapters 14 and 15.*
BRASSINGTON AND PETTITT: *Chapter 18.*
KOTLER, ARMSTRONG, SAUNDERS AND WONG: *Chapter 22.*
BLYTHE (2006): *Chapter 19.*

18	
sales promotion	

Sales promotion is an activity which is intended to give a temporary boost to sales. The Institute of Sales Promotion (www.isp.org.uk) defines it as:

> A range of tactical marketing techniques designed within a strategic marketing framework to add value to a product or service in order to achieve specific sales and marketing objectives.

'Tactical' means short-term, although sales promotions can build longer-term sales. Sales promotion can be:

1. ***Manufacturer promotions:*** the manufacturer promotes to the end consumer, to pull sales through the distribution network.

2. ***Trade promotions:*** the manufacturer (or wholesaler) promotes to a distributor in order to push product through the distribution network.

3. ***Retailer promotions:*** the retailer promotes to the consumer in order to push the product out of the shop.

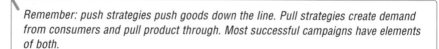

Remember: push strategies push goods down the line. Pull strategies create demand from consumers and pull product through. Most successful campaigns have elements of both.

Sales promotions have the following effects:

1. They increase stock levels in the distribution chain.

2. They encourage members of the chain to give the product more prominence in store.

3. They even out fluctuating sales, for example due to seasonality.

4 They often shut out the competition.

5 For retailers, they increase store traffic, which improves sales of other goods.

6 They increase frequency and amount of purchase.

7 They can increase store loyalty – depending on the promotion.

8 They can increase own-brand sales.

9 They can encourage trials of new products.

10 They expand usage of the product.

11 They attract new customers.

12 They can encourage customers to 'trade up' to a more expensive version.

13 They encourage consumers to 'load up' with the product.

Most sales promotions only result in a temporary switch of brands. Consumers switch back again as soon as the promotion ends.

You are likely to be asked about specific sales promotion techniques as well as the effects the sales promotion is expected to have. The problem here is that there is a wide range of techniques: in general, though, they fall into these categories:

1 **Price promotions:** this includes buy-one-get-one-free and extra-fill promotions.

2 *Prize promotions:* either the consumer collects proof of purchase, or there is a scratch card or similar which comes with the pack. In the UK, it is illegal to require someone to buy the product in order to enter the draw.

3 *Self-liquidating offers:* a self-liquidating offer is one in which consumers can buy another product at a discount provided they have proof of purchase on the product being promoted.

4 *Loyalty schemes:* there is some debate as to whether these are sales promotions or not, since they do not produce a temporary increase in sales, but rather generate a long-term level of loyalty.

Sales promotions seldom work alone. They need to be integrated into the overall marketing strategy, and need to be supported by advertising and sometimes PR as well. Trade promotions will require the support and cooperation of the salesforce, who will of course equally be supported by the promotion.

Sales promotions carry with them some dangers. These are as follows:

1 A sales promotion can devalue the brand: consumers sometimes wonder why the company feels the need to discount its products in this way.

2 If the promotion is repeated too often, people come to expect it and will hold back from buying until the promotion returns. This can be seriously counter-productive.

3 Sales promotions cut into profits: in particular price promotions can seriously hurt margins.

4 It can be difficult to gauge the level of the response ahead of time – there have been some spectacular PR blunders through firms being unable to meet the demand for a popular promotion.

Promotions can sometimes be carried out in conjunction with another firm: this will reduce the cost and the risk. Such promotions work best when the other firm has a product which is complementary, for example giving away free samples of coffee whitener on jars of instant coffee, or giving away free writing paper with expensive pens.

Whenever you are asked to consider running a sales promotion, begin by imagining how the consumer will use the product. This will help you focus on deciding what other products might be appropriate to offer alongside the product being promoted.

As always in marketing, you should try to compete on something other than price if at all possible. Adding value is almost always better than cutting profit.

Taking it *FURTHER*

The value of sales promotions is somewhat doubtful. They do not lead to permanent brand switching in most cases. They do not increase sales over the year as a whole (because people stock up while the promotion is on, then simply live on their stocks when the promotion ends). They often damage brand values, and they always cut profit margins to some extent.

If the firm is to make any real permanent gains from the promotion, managers may need to be a little bit more creative. For example, in a self-liquidating promotion, the company will presumably gain a mailing list, which has some value. Sales promotions can be used for market research, for test marketing, for salesforce support, and for customer retention. All it needs is for the managers to think!

Here is a sample exam question.

"How might you mitigate the dangers of too big a response to a sales promotion?"

To answer this, you would be expected to be able to say something about predicting possible demand. You then need to consider possible ways of avoiding disaster! Putting 'While stocks last!' on the offer is a start, but it is really not a good idea to annoy customers who have perhaps carefully collected their packet tops and now expect their free teddy beer. You need to ensure that further promotional products can be obtained, at short notice if possible, and you should have a system ready to write to people and explain that there may be a delay, but they will get the goods.

Another possibility is that you will be asked to show how sales promotion fits into the communication mix. For example:

❝What are the advantages and disadvantages of sales promotion compared with other elements of the marketing mix?❞

Sales promotion is intended to produce an instant, measurable response and in that respect it is entirely different from advertising or PR. It is an impersonal, mass medium unlike selling, so it is able to produce results very quickly. It therefore has the advantage of being able to produce a 'quick fix' for falls in sales, or to even out seasonality, in a much more predictable way than the other mix elements. The main drawbacks are that it is expensive compared with advertising or PR. It only moves sales forward in most cases, and it does not usually produce a permanent increase in sales.

Textbook guide

ADCOCK, HALBORG AND ROSS: *Chapter 18.*
JOBBER: *Chapter 16.*
BRASSINGTON AND PETTITT: *Chapter 16.*
KOTLER, ARMSTRONG, SAUNDERS AND WONG: *Chapter 19.*
BLYTHE (2006): *Chapter 18.*

19

managing channels of distribution

Distributors perform a number of necessary functions, not least of which is that they place the product where the consumer can get at it. Distributors include wholesalers, retailers, agents, factors, and many other types of intermediary.

The basis of distribution is the concept of the value chain. A value chain is the group of firms which handle the product through from raw materials to the end product.

The end product of a value chain is a satisfied consumer.

Each member of the value chain adds value to the process, otherwise they would be bypassed by the other members of the chain: although cutting out the middle man is popularly supposed to be a way of cutting prices, it actually reduces efficiency and therefore would tend to raise costs and consequently prices.

Overall, the value chain shows a profit: the share of the profit which each member gets is a subject for negotiation, and for the exercise of power by the more powerful members. Managing the value chain is a complex affair, but if the chain is managed well it will be more efficient and every member will benefit in the long run. This is harder to achieve than might at first appear, because of course each member has more to gain in the short term by being difficult than by co-operating.

Intermediaries are useful for the following reasons:

1 They add transactional value. Because the intermediary is closer to the customers, and can offer the same customer products from a number of different producers, the transactions move more smoothly.

2 They add logistical value. It is simpler for the customers to go to one place to buy everything than it would be to go to a lot of different producers. Equally, for a producer of, say, canned tuna, to deliver a few cases of fish to every small grocer in the country would be incredibly inefficient – a food wholesaler can deliver a lorry load of items from different manufacturers in one drop.

3 They add facilitating value. Intermediaries take on some of the risk, and also provide some of the financing by holding stocks of the products.

All these functions would have to be performed by someone – it is simply more efficient for them to be carried out by specialist intermediaries than for each producer to try to do them alone.

Market coverage might be selective (using only a few outlets in a given area), intensive (distributing as widely as possible in the area) or exclusive (using perhaps only one outlet in a given area). The choice of coverage depends on the product and on agreements with distributors: many prefer to have exclusive rights so as not to have to compete with other distributors.

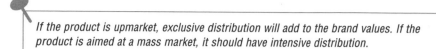

> *If the product is upmarket, exclusive distribution will add to the brand values. If the product is aimed at a mass market, it should have intensive distribution.*

Power in the value chain might be concentrated at any level. In many chains, the retailers hold the power, so manufacturers have to do as they are told. In some value chains the wholesalers, importer or even the manufacturers might hold the power.

For most manufacturers, getting the right distribution is the key to success, because without distribution the product will go nowhere. Unfortunately, few manufacturers really have the choice of where and when to distribute.

Within the value chain, conflict is likely. Sources of power in the chain can be:

1 *Economic:* size of firm, control of resources, shareholdings in the other members of the chain, or coercive power all come under this category.

2 *Non-economic sources:* expert power (one firm has skills the others need), and reward power (the ability to provide benefits to other members) come under this category.

One firm may be more willing than the others to take the lead, or may have a high level of power derived from the factors above.

Channel management techniques include the following:

1 *Refusal to deal:* in most countries, firms do not have to sell to any-body if they don't want to. There may be a legal problem if refusal to deal is used as a punishment against a firm which has refused to cooperate in an unfair practice.

2 *Tying contracts:* the supplier insists that the distributor carries a full range of the supplier's products. Most of these contracts are illegal, but there are exceptions, notably in **franchise** deals or if the supplier's goods are of a specific quality (for example, if the supplier insists that the distributor carries a full range of spare parts).

3 *Exclusive dealing:* a retailer might insist that no other retailer can carry exactly the same model. This is common practice in consumer durables: this is how retailers can give 'price promises'. They know the product is not available anywhere else.

4 *Restricted sales territories:* manufacturers can insist that distributors do not sell outside their own territory. This protects other distributors, so most are happy to go along with it since they are being protected themselves. Sometimes courts view this as a restrictive practice, however.

> *Using excessive power in controlling a distributor may be seen as a restrictive trade practice, which will land the company in court.*

Sometimes there is competition within the channels themselves. One retailer may compete with another, or a wholesaler might compete with a retailer by dealing direct with the public. The Internet has increased the propensity for this to happen: for example, publishers sometimes have websites from which they sell books direct to the public. Retailers are unlikely to have a problem with this unless the publishers start to undercut the retailers – but since booksellers by and large do not feel threatened by Amazon, which takes pride in undercutting them, the Internet is obviously not about to upset the system just yet.

Value chains can be more or less integrated. Vertically integrated chains are those which are strongly cohesive from raw materials through to final consumer. Horizontal integration refers to cooperation, collusion or merger across a single level of the chain. For example, the oil business is vertically integrated: from exploration through to the petrol pumps, the same firms control everything. On the other hand, the newspaper industry is horizontally integrated, with relatively few newspaper publishers and only one or two wholesale distributors handling the whole industry.

Taking a **logistics** viewpoint means considering the value chain as a complete unit, rather than a set of separate businesses each jockeying for position. Making the logistics flow smoothly benefits everybody in the long run: the only discussion remaining is how to divide the profits!

A recent extension of the logistics approach is efficient customer response (ECR) which is a computer-moderated system for making the value chain work more effectively. The features are:

1 *Continuous replenishment:* the supplier plans production on the basis of information supplied by the retailer.

2 *Cross-docking:* the suppliers' and retailers' trucks arrive at the distribution centre as nearly as possible at the same time, so that goods go straight from one to the other without going into storage at all.

3 *Roll-cage sequencing:* goods are stored by category at the warehouse, which saves time for the retailer (though it adds to the work for the warehouse).

Taking it **FURTHER**

Distribution is seen by non-marketers as being an unnecessary extra expense. Cutting out the middle man is a cliché: yet obviously distributors do some good, or they would quickly disappear.

Going further, though, distributors can actually become part of the benefits of the product. What about exclusive retailers like Harrods? Or the door-to-door service provided by Avon Cosmetics? Can distribution be seen as a part of the communications package, giving a message to the consumers?

This is another example of the ways in which marketing mix activities spill over into each other.

Questions on distribution are likely to involve logistics and the value chain. You will need to consider how any strategic distribution decisions deliver added value (and added satisfaction) to the consumers. Here are two sample questions:

"Under what circumstances would a firm want to use exclusive distribution? What effect might this have on the rest of the value chain?"

Firms might want exclusive distribution in circumstances where the product is itself exclusive. The added value for the end consumer comes from the pleasure of knowing that not everyone can have the particular product: self-esteem and prestige needs are being met. The effect on the value chain is that overall profit margins are likely to be much higher, and although the logistics might be more complicated, ultimately the whole chain should benefit in terms of greater profit from lower volume of goods.

"Why do products such as canned tuna typically have longer distribution chains than products such as home improvements?"

The point with this question is that canned tuna is a cheap, regular purchase while home improvements are expensive and infrequently purchased. Because each member of the value chain adds value and improves efficiency, cheap products often use longer chains: home improvements are tailored to the customer, and therefore need a short chain.

Textbook guide

ADCOCK, HALBORG AND ROSS: *Chapter 13.*
JOBBER: *Chapter 17.*
BRASSINGTON AND PETTITT: *Chapters 12 and 13.*
KOTLER, ARMSTRONG, SAUNDERS AND WONG: *Chapter 21.*
BLYTHE (2006): *Chapters 20 and 21.*

20	
services marketing: people, processes, physical evidence	

Services and physical products are probably not as far apart conceptually as is popularly supposed. Either one provides benefits to the consumer, and in some cases the same benefits can be provided by either a service or a physical product. A special birthday treat for a boyfriend might be a meal out (a service) or a bottle of single malt whisky (a physical product). Since virtually all physical products have a service element, and virtually all services have a physical element, the distinction may be arbitrary and artificial.

However, there is not much argument that some products are more physical than others, and so services marketing has become a way of explaining how to market products which are at the 'service' end of the spectrum.

The service element of products has become of much greater importance to the economy in recent years. For example, 40 years ago the majority of people rarely ate meals outside the home (apart from lunch in the works canteen). Food had a very limited service element – people cooked meals from basic ingredients. In the twenty-first century, most people eat out at least once a month, often much more, and even when they eat at home it is often a ready meal prepared by someone else.

Given the importance of services in post-industrial society (hardly anybody earns their living by making things, at least in Britain) you are likely to be able to bring in something about services marketing into many exam questions. You are also likely to have assignments on services marketing: you may even study a specialist course on the topic.

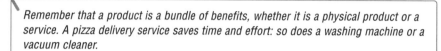

Remember that a product is a bundle of benefits, whether it is a physical product or a service. A pizza delivery service saves time and effort: so does a washing machine or a vacuum cleaner.

A pure service has the following characteristics:

1 *Intangibility:* services cannot be touched.

2 *Perishability:* for example, an aeroplane seat cannot be sold once the plane has taken off.

3 *Heterogeneity:* services vary a lot – a grumpy flight attendant can spoil your trip!

4 *Inseparability:* production and consumption happen at the same time – you enjoy the flight while it is happening, not before or after.

5 *Lack of ownership:* you can't sell a haircut second-hand.

Because services are provided by people, the people in the equation are an important factor. The designers at Ford may or may not be nice people to talk to, but that doesn't matter to a Ford owner: whether your hairdresser is nice to talk to makes a big difference!

Aer Lingus say that they don't train their staff in customer relations. They just hire nice people to start with.

SERVICES MARKETING | *111*

Process differs between different services. A ready-packaged hamburger from the supermarket is different from a hamburger from a burger restaurant, which is different again from a Vienna steak in a posh restaurant. The process is different in each case, even though the physical element is almost identical.

Physical evidence is proof that the service took place. This could be in the form of brochures, the physical surroundings in which the service happens, the physical element of the product (the food, the aircraft, and so on), or documentary evidence such as an insurance policy document.

> *People, process and physical evidence are the differentiators in service industries. They are what make the individual firm stand out.*

The major problem for the consumer is that services cannot be tested before being consumed, and (perhaps more importantly) before being paid for. Word of mouth therefore plays a much greater role in services markets. In some cases suppliers like restaurants do not get paid until after the service has been consumed, so waiters will check part-way through the meal if everything is all right: even if it isn't, the customer who says 'Fine, thanks!' will have difficulty wriggling out of paying later!

Measuring service quality is a complex area, because services vary anyway, even from one customer to another.

> *Because the customer is involved in the creation of the service, there will always be variability.*

Parasuraman, Zeithaml and Berry (1985) created the SERVQUAL model as a way of assessing service quality. SERVQUAL measures against ten criteria:

1 **Access:** how easy is it to access the service?

2 **Reliability:** does the service always happen the way it should?

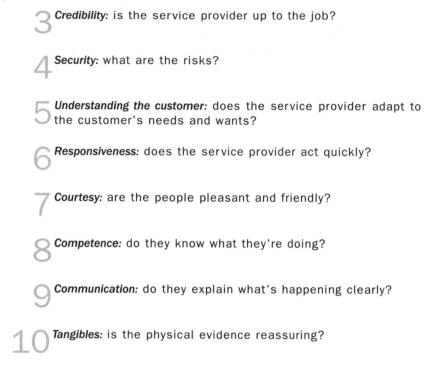

3 *Credibility:* is the service provider up to the job?

4 *Security:* what are the risks?

5 *Understanding the customer:* does the service provider adapt to the customer's needs and wants?

6 *Responsiveness:* does the service provider act quickly?

7 *Courtesy:* are the people pleasant and friendly?

8 *Competence:* do they know what they're doing?

9 *Communication:* do they explain what's happening clearly?

10 *Tangibles:* is the physical evidence reassuring?

The first five elements relate to outcomes; the second five relate to inputs.

SERVQUAL has been widely criticised: for one thing, most of the elements are subjective, and second some of the elements would be almost impossible to verify (for example, a staff member might normally be extremely courteous, but faced with an aggressive, swearing customer might become equally aggressive:

According to Parasuraman et al., there are four barriers to service quality, all the fault of the supplier:

1 *Misconceptions:* not understanding the customer's needs.

2 *Inadequate resources:* too few staff, too poor an environment, etc.

3 *Inadequate delivery:* staff who are incompetent cannot deliver the service effectively.

4 *Exaggerated promises:* because the service cannot be assessed by consumers before it is bought, it is tempting for suppliers to exaggerate the benefits.

Taking _{it} **FURTHER**

Services are the future, but they are expensive to provide because people are expensive to employ. Most of a firm's overheads are walking around on two legs! So naturally there has been a shift towards automating service provision. The travel industry is an example – customers are expected to use the Internet to make their bookings, not go through a travel agent. Even if they telephone the airline or ferry company, they are usually met with an automated telephonist who asks them to 'press one for a new booking, press two to amend a booking, press three for any other enquiry'. Having pressed three, the customer is probably connected to a call centre in Delhi anyway.

For service providers, the temptation to reduce service levels in order to cut costs is great, and in some cases it has worked (low-cost airlines, for example). In most cases, Western consumers are sufficiently wealthy not to want to put up with reduced service – how many people would be prepared to stay in a hotel without en-suite bathrooms, for instance? Yet that was the norm 30 years ago.

Rising expectations and rising standards of living mean that service employees want more money, too. So where will it all end? Can we all make a living opening doors for each other?

Exam questions on services are likely to centre around the 7P model, although SERVQUAL may enter into the equation. Because services marketing is often tacked on to marketing courses, almost as an afterthought, you may be asked to contrast services marketing with physical product marketing. For example:

" It has been said that services marketing is not essentially different from marketing physical products. Why might this be so? "

You would need to begin by discussing the similarities between marketing services and marketing physical products, for example, that a product is a bundle of benefits. You would then need to point out some of the differences (while keeping to the point that all products are combinations of services and physical product). The problem is essentially one of definition – when does a product cease to be defined as a physical product and become defined as a service product, and vice-versa?

Sometimes you might be asked to explain the differentiators in services marketing. For example:

"What are the key factors which differentiate one service provider from another?"

The answer actually comes in two parts: at the conceptual level, it is the people, processes and physical evidence which distinguish one firm from another. At the practical level, firms differentiate themselves by differences in service levels, by differences in staff empowerment, and by differences in service outcomes.

Textbook guide

ADCOCK, HALBORG AND ROSS: *Chapter 11.*
JOBBER: *Chapter 21.*
BRASSINGTON AND PETTITT: *Chapter 22.*
KOTLER, ARMSTRONG, SAUNDERS AND WONG: *Chapter 15.*
BLYTHE (2006): *Chapter 22.*

21	
marketing ethics	

Some textbooks have separate chapters on ethics (notably American texts, where it is a requirement), whereas others deal with ethical issues as they arise within the separate topics.

Ethical behaviour is about doing the right thing for the benefit of other people, rather than the thing which is of benefit to yourself. The problem lies in defining what is acceptable and what is not: for example, people expect a certain amount of exaggeration in advertising, but do not expect outright lies, but defining the line at which one becomes the other is not at all simple. Two basic ethical theories apply: **teleology,** which implies that behaviour should be judged by its outcomes (the ends justify the means), and **deontology,** which states that actions are ethical or not, independently of outcome: deontology seeks the greatest good of the greatest number.

Examples of ethical problems which marketers are accused of are as follows:

1 Salespeople using high-pressure techniques to persuade people to buy something they do not really need.

2 Companies selling shoddy or unsafe products.

3 **Planned obsolescence.**

4 Differential pricing.

5 Giving poorer service to people who have no choice.

6 Encouraging materialism.

7 Cultural pollution: this has been called the McDonaldisation of the world.

8 Environmental damage caused by over-consumption.

9 Encouraging 'pester power' by marketing to children.

10 Bribery to buyers.

There are, of course, counter forces at work to reduce unethical behaviour. These are:

1 Consumer movements, including environmentalism.

2 Legislation.

3 Consumers simply voting with their feet, and refusing to buy from unethical companies.

4 Employees 'whistle-blowing' to the media.

5 Consumer journalism.

> *The old adage that fair exchange is not robbery applies. Defining fairness is, however, subjective!*

Naturally, the interests of the consumers and the interests of the firm are not identical, but a marketing orientation implies that the good of the firm ultimately relies on the good of the consumers.

> *Research shows that people can have one set of morals in the workplace, and a different set of morals at home.*

A hundred and fifty years ago, marketing ethics could be simply summed up as 'caveat emptor', which means 'buyer beware'. People were expected to check things for themselves, and not rely on the seller to ensure that products were safe and good value. This was probably fine for people buying cabbages, but the complexity of modern products means that it is impossible for the average consumer to judge whether the product is up to standard or not. There are several views on the degree to which marketers should become involved in ethical questions:

1 The company has a responsibility for its products and employees: all must meet customer expectations, regardless of legislation or outside pressure.

2 The company's responsibility is to stay within the law, and respond to reasonable requests from pressure groups.

3 The company's responsibility is to its staff and shareholders. If the law threatens this, the company should lobby or find loopholes in order to survive.

Establishing an ethical company is not straightforward, because organisations are formed of individuals, who each have their own beliefs about what is ethical and what is not. Some companies lay down ethical standards in their corporate vision or mission statement, and find it is ignored by the staff: others empower middle managers (or even grassroots employees) to act as their consciences dictate, and find that the result is a complete shambles, with widespread inconsistencies.

Taking it **FURTHER**

Some companies (and people, of course) only act ethically when they have no other choice. Others have a strong sense of right and wrong. The question is: to what extent should businesses think in terms of ethics, and to what extent should they think in terms of practicality? In the last analysis, is there really a difference?

For example, many industries have trade associations which act in a self-regulatory manner. These trade associations have usually been set up in response to threats from government that, if the industry does not clean up its act, there will be legislation. Examples are the Time Share Association, the Double Glazing Federation, and the British Board of Film Censors.

Is this really different from the way individuals learn ethical behaviour, though? If we behave badly, other people tell us to behave better, and eventually most of us learn to fit in. We are not naturally moral people – we learn it, by being punished when we put a foot wrong. So why should companies be any different?

Exam questions commonly present students with an ethical dilemma to solve. For example:

"Your firm manufactures power tools. You discover a major fault in a popular power saw that could prove dangerous to the user in a tiny minority of cases, but recalling the product would probably bankrupt the company, putting hundreds of people out of work. So far the fault has not actually manifested itself, and considering the normal domestic use of a power saw may never arise. What do you do?"

There are two elements to this question: the philosophical and ethical position, and the practical and legal issues. Philosophically and ethically, you have on the one hand a situation where the welfare of hundreds of people is set against the hypothetical risk to a few people, so a deontologist might argue that the greatest good of the greatest number lies in doing nothing, especially since bankrupting the company will not fix the saws. The practical and legal position says that if someone is injured by the product, and the company knew the risks, a lawsuit will follow which might itself bankrupt the company.

You would be expected to argue the case from the different ethical positions: the final decision is, of course, down to your conscience! Another example might be:

"You are a sales representative for an office-equipment manufacturer. As your presentation progresses with one particular client, you realise that the client has made an assumption about your product which is not, in fact, true. The client clearly regards this untrue aspect of the product as being very attractive, and is planning on buying the product on the basis of a non-existent feature. On the other hand, you know that the product is perfect for this customer and you would not want them to buy your competitor's inferior model. What should you do?"

The obvious answer is that you should tell the client of the mistake, but of course there are many salespeople who would not do so. The greatest good for the customer is in fact to buy the product, so the salesperson should correct the misunderstanding, but continue with the presentation and let the facts speak for themselves.

You would probably gain some extra marks by pointing out that, in this case, the customer will find out about the misunderstanding when the equipment is delivered anyway, and is not likely to be forgiving!

Textbook guide

ADCOCK, HALBORG AND ROSS: *Chapter 24.*
JOBBER: *each chapter has a section on ethics.*
BRASSINGTON AND PETTITT: *Chapter 2, but with references throughout the book.*
KOTLER, ARMSTRONG, SAUNDERS AND WONG: *Chapter 2.*
BLYTHE (2006): *Chapters 3 and 11, but with references throughout the book.*

part three

study, writing and revision
skills (in collaboration with
David McIllroy)

General introduction

If you work your way carefully through this chapter you should at the
end be better equipped to profit from your lectures, benefit from your
seminars, construct your essays efficiently, develop effective revision
strategies and respond comprehensively to the pressures of exam situations. In the five sections that lie ahead you will be presented with:
checklists and bullet points to focus your attention on key issues; exercises to help you participate actively in the learning experience; illustrations and analogies to enable you to anchor learning principles in
everyday events and experiences; worked examples to demonstrate the
use of such features as structure, headings and continuity; tips that provide practical advice in nutshell form.

In the exercises that are presented each student should decide how
much effort they would like to invest in each exercise, according to individual preferences and requirements. Some of the points in the exercises
will be covered in the text either before or after the exercise. You might
prefer to read each section right through before going back to tackle the
exercises. Suggested answers are provided after some of the exercises, so
avoid these if you prefer to work through the exercises on your own. The

aim is to prompt you to reflect on the material, remember what you have read and trigger you to add your own thoughts. Space is provided for you to write your responses down in a few words, or you may prefer to reflect on them within your own mind. However, writing will help you to slow down and digest the material and may also enable you to process the information at a deeper level of learning.

Finally, the overall aim of the chapter is to point you to the keys for academic and personal development. The twin emphases of academic development and personal qualities are stressed throughout. By giving attention to these factors you will give yourself the toolkit you will need to excel in your studies.

1

how to get the most out of your lectures

This section will show you how to:

- Make the most of your lecture notes.
- Prepare your mind for new terms.
- Develop an independent approach to learning.
- Write efficient summary notes from lectures.
- Take the initiative in building on your lectures.

Keeping in context

According to higher educational commentators and advisors, best quality learning is facilitated when it is set within an overall learning context. It should be the responsibility of your tutors to provide a context for you to learn in, but it is your responsibility to see the overall context, and you can do this even before your first lecture begins. Such a panoramic view can be achieved by becoming familiar with the outline content of both a given subject and the entire study programme. Before you go into each lecture you should briefly remind yourself of where it fits into the overall scheme of things. Think, for example, of how much more confident you feel when you move into a new city (e.g. to attend university) once you become familiar with your bearings – namely where you live in relation to college, shops, stores, buses, trains, places of entertainment, and so on.

The same principle applies to your course – find your way around your study programme and locate the position of each lecture within this overall framework.

Use of lecture notes

It is always beneficial to do some preliminary reading before you enter a lecture. If lecture notes are provided in advance (for example, electronically), then print these out, read over them and bring them with you to the lecture. You can insert question marks on issues where you will need further clarification. Some lecturers prefer to provide full notes, some prefer to make skeleton outlines available and some prefer to issue no notes at all! If notes are provided, take full advantage and supplement these with your own notes as you listen. In a later section on memory techniques you see that humans possess an ability for 're-learning savings' – namely it is easier to learn material the second time round, as it is evident that we have a capacity to hold residual memory deposits. So some basic preparation will equip you with a great advantage – you will be able to 'tune in' and think more clearly about the lecture than you would have done with the preliminary work.

If you set yourself too many tedious tasks in the early stages of your academic programme you may lose some motivation and momentum. A series of short, simple, achievable tasks can give your mind the 'lubrication' you need. For example, you are more likely to maintain preliminary reading for a lecture if you set modest targets.

Mastering technical terms

Let us assume that in an early lecture you are introduced to a series of new terms such as 'paradigm', 'empirical' and 'zeitgeist'. If you are hearing these and other terms for the first time, you could end up with a headache! New words can be threatening, especially if you have to face a string of them in one lecture. The uncertainty about the new terms may impair your ability to benefit fully from the lecture and therefore hinder the quality of your learning. Some subjects require technical terms and the use of them is unavoidable. However, when you have heard a term a number of times it will not seem as daunting as it initially was. It is claimed that individuals may have particular strengths in the scope of their vocabulary. Some people may have a good recognition vocabulary – they immediately know what a word means when they read it or hear it in context. Others have a good command of language when they speak – they have an ability to recall words freely. Still others are more fluent in recall when they write – words seem to flow rapidly for them when they engage in the dynamics of writing. You can work at developing all three approaches in your course, and the checklist below may be of some help in mastering and marshalling the terms you hear in lectures.

In terms of learning new words, it will be very useful if you can first try to work out what they mean from their context when you first encounter them. You might be much better at this than you imagine, especially if there is only one word in the sentence that you do not understand. It would also be very useful if you could obtain a small indexed notebook and use this to build up your own glossary of terms. In this way you could include a definition of a word, an example of its use, where it fits into a theory and any practical application of it.

Checklist for mastering terms used in your lectures:

- ✓ Read lecture notes before the lectures and list any unfamiliar terms.
- ✓ Read over the listed terms until you are familiar with their sound.
- ✓ Try to work out meanings of terms from their context.
- ✓ Do not suspend learning the meaning of a term indefinitely.
- ✓ Write out a sentence that includes the new word (do this for each word).
- ✓ Meet with other students and test each other with the technical terms.
- ✓ Jot down new words you hear in lectures and check out the meaning soon afterwards.

Your confidence will greatly increase when you begin to follow the flow of arguments that contain technical terms, and more especially when you can freely use the terms yourself in speaking and writing.

Developing independent study

In the current educational ethos there are the twin aims of cultivating teamwork/group activities and independent learning. There is not necessarily a conflict between the two, as they should complement each other. For example, if you are committed to independent learning you have more to offer other students when you work in small groups, and you will also be prompted to follow up on the leads given by them. Furthermore, the guidelines given to you in lectures are designed to lead you into deeper independent study. The issues raised in lectures are pointers to provide direction and structure for your extended personal pursuit. Your aim should invariably be to build on what you are given, and you should never think of merely returning the bare bones of the lecture material in a coursework essay or exam.

It is always very refreshing to a marker to be given work from a student that contains recent studies that the examiner had not previously encountered.

Note taking strategy

Note taking in lectures is an art that you will only perfect with practice and by trial and error. Each student should find the formula that works best for him or her. What works for one, does not work for the other. Some students can write more quickly than others, some are better at shorthand than others and some are better at deciphering their own scrawl! The problem will always be to try to find a balance between concentrating beneficially on what you hear, with making sufficient notes that will enable you to comprehend later what you have heard. You should not, however, become frustrated by the fact that you will not understand or remember immediately everything you have heard.

By being present at a lecture, and by making some attempt to attend to what you hear, you will already have a substantial advantage over those students who do not attend.

Guidelines for note taking in lectures:

- Develop the note taking strategy that works best for you.
- Work at finding a balance between listening and writing.
- Make some use of optimal shorthand (for example, a few key words may summarise a story).
- Too much writing may impair the flow of the lecture for you.
- Too much writing may impair the quality of your notes.
- Some limited notes are better than none.
- Good note taking may facilitate deeper processing of information.
- It is essential to 'tidy up' notes as soon as possible after a lecture.
- Reading over notes soon after lectures will consolidate your learning.

Developing the lecture

Some educationalists have criticised the value of lectures because they allege that these are a mode of merely 'passive learning'. This can certainly be an accurate conclusion to arrive at (that is, if students approach lectures in the wrong way) and lecturers can work to devise ways of making lectures more interactive. For example, they can make use of interactive handouts or by posing questions during the lecture and giving time out for students to reflect on these. Other possibilities are short discussions at given junctures in the lecture or use of small groups within the session. As a student you do not have to enter a lecture in passive mode and you can ensure that you are not merely a passive recipient of information by taking steps to develop the lecture yourself. A list of suggestions is presented below to help you take the initiative in developing the lecture content.

Checklist to ensure that the lecture is not merely a passive experience:

- ✓ Try to interact with the lecture material by asking questions.
- ✓ Highlight points that you would like to develop in personal study.
- ✓ Trace connections between the lecture and other parts of your study programme.
- ✓ Bring together notes from the lecture and other sources.
- ✓ Restructure the lecture outline into your own preferred format.
- ✓ Think of ways in which aspects of the lecture material can be applied.
- ✓ Design ways in which aspects of the lecture material can be illustrated.
- ✓ If the lecturer invites questions, make a note of all the questions asked.
- ✓ Follow up on issues of interest that have arisen out of the lecture.

You can contribute to this active involvement in a lecture by engaging with the material before, during and after it is delivered.

You might now like to attempt to summarise (and/or add) some factors that would help you to capitalise fully on the benefits of a lecture.

✓ ....

✓ ....

✓ ....

✓ ....

✓ ....

2	
how to make the most of seminars	

This section will show you how to:

- Be aware of the value of seminars.
- Focus on links to learning.
- Recognise qualities you can use repeatedly.
- Manage potential problems in seminars.
- Prepare yourself adequately for seminars.

Not to be underestimated

Seminars are often optional in a degree programme and sometimes poorly attended because they are underestimated. Some students may be convinced that the lecture is the truly authoritative way to receive quality information. Undoubtedly, lectures play an important role in an academic programme, but seminars have a unique contribution to learning that will complement lectures. Other students may feel that their time would be better spent in personal study. Again, private study is unquestionably essential for personal learning and development, but you will nevertheless diminish your learning experience if you neglect seminars. If seminars were to be removed from academic programmes, then something really important would be lost.

Checklist – some useful features of seminars:

- ✓ Can identify problems that you had not thought of.
- ✓ Can clear up confusing issues.
- ✓ Allows you to ask questions and make comments.
- ✓ Can help you develop friendships and teamwork.
- ✓ Enables you to refresh and consolidate your knowledge.
- ✓ Can help you sharpen motivation and redirect study efforts.

An asset to complement other learning activities

In higher education at the present time there is emphasis on variety – variety in delivery, learning experience, learning styles and assessment methods. The seminar is deemed to hold an important place within the overall scheme of teaching, learning and assessment. In some programmes the seminars are directly linked to the assessment task. Whether or not they have such a place in your course, they will provide you with a unique opportunity to learn and develop.

In a seminar you will hear a variety of contributions, and different perspectives and emphases. You will have the chance to interrupt and the experience of being interrupted! You will also learn that you can get things wrong and still survive! It is often the case that when one student admits that they did not know some important piece of information, other students quickly follow on to the same admission in the wake of this. If you can learn to ask questions and not feel stupid, then seminars will give you an asset for learning and a life-long educational quality.

Creating the right climate in seminars

It has been said that we have been given only one mouth to talk, but two ears to listen. One potential problem with seminars is that some students may take a while to learn this lesson, and other students may have to help hasten them on the way (graciously but firmly!). In lectures your main role is to listen and take notes, but in seminars there is the challenge to strike the balance between listening and speaking. It is important to make a beginning in speaking even if it is just to repeat something that you agree with. You can also learn to disagree in an agreeable way. For example, you can raise a question against what someone else has said and pose this in a good tone – for example, 'If that is the case, does that not mean that ...'. In addition it is perfectly possible to disagree with others by avoiding personal attacks, such as, 'that was a really stupid thing to say', or 'I thought you knew better than that', or 'I'm surprised that you don't know that by now'. Educationalists say that it is important to have the right climate to learn in, and the avoidance of unnecessary conflict will foster such a climate.

EXERCISE

Suggest what can be done to reach agreement (set ground rules) that would help keep seminars running smoothly and harmoniously.

✓ ....

✓ ....

✓ ....

✓ ....

✓ ....

Some suggestions are: appoint someone to guide and control the discussion; invite individuals to prepare in advance to make a contribution; hand out agreed discussion questions at some point prior to the seminar; stress at the beginning that no one should monopolise the discussion and emphasise that there must be no personal attacks on any individual (state clearly what this means). Also you could invite and encourage quieter students to participate and assure each person that their contribution is valued.

Links in learning and transferable skills

An important principle in learning to progress from shallow to deep learning is developing the capacity to make connecting links between themes or topics and across subjects. This also applies to the various learning activities such as lectures, seminars, fieldwork, computer searches and private study. Another factor to think about is, 'what skills can I develop, or improve on, from seminars that I can use across my study programme?' A couple of examples of key skills are the ability to communicate and the capacity to work within a team. These are skills that you will be able to use at various points in your course (transferable), but you are not likely to develop them within the formal setting of a lecture.

EXERCISE

Write out or think about (a) three things that give seminars value, and, (b) three useful skills that you can develop in seminars.

(a)

✓ ....

✓ ....

✓ ....

(b)

✓ ....

✓ ....

✓ ....

In the above exercises, for (a) you could have – variety of contributors, flexibility to spend more time on problematic issues and an agreed agenda settled at the beginning of the seminar. For (b) you could have, communication, conflict resolution and team work.

A key question that you should bring to every seminar – 'How does this seminar connect with my other learning activities and my assessments?'

An opportunity to contribute

If you have never made a contribution to a seminar before, you may need something to use as an 'ice breaker'. It does not matter if your first contribution is only a sentence of two – the important thing is to make a start. One way to do this is to make brief notes as others contribute, and whilst doing this, a question or two might arise in your mind. If your first contribution is a question, that is a good start. Or it may be that you will be able to point out some connection between what others have said, or identify conflicting opinions that need to be resolved. If you have already begun making contributions, it is important that you keep the momentum going, and do not allow yourself to lapse back into the safe cocoon of shyness.

EXERCISE

See if you can suggest how you might resolve some of the following problems that might hinder you from making a contribution to seminars.

One student who dominates and monopolises the discussion.

✓ ....

✓ ....

Someone else has already said what you really want to say.

✓ ....

✓ ....

Fear that someone else will correct you and make you feel stupid.

✓ ....

✓ ....

Feel that your contribution might be seen as short and shallow.

✓ ....

✓ ....

A previous negative experience puts you off making any more contributions.

✓ ....

✓ ....

Strategies for benefiting from your seminar experience

If you are required to bring a presentation to your seminar, you might want to consult a full chapter on presentations in a complementary study guide (McIlroy, 2003). Alternatively, you may be content with the summary bullet points presented at the end of this section. In order to benefit from discussions in seminars (the focus of this chapter), some useful summary nutshells are now presented as a checklist.

Checklist – how to benefit from seminars:

✓ Do some preparatory reading.
✓ Familiarise yourself with the main ideas to be addressed.
✓ Make notes during the seminar.
✓ Make some verbal contribution, even a question.
✓ Remind yourself of the skills you can develop.
✓ Trace learning links from the seminar to other subjects/topics on your programme.
✓ Make brief bullet points on what you should follow up on.
✓ Read over your notes as soon as possible after the seminar.
✓ Continue discussion with fellow students after the seminar has ended.

If required to give a presentation:

• Have a practice run with friends.
• If using visuals, do not obstruct them.
• Check out beforehand that all equipment works.
• Space out points clearly on visuals (large and legible).
• Time talk by visuals (for example, 5 slides by 15 minute talk = 3 minutes per slide).
• Make sure your talk synchronises with the slide on view at any given point.

- Project your voice so that everyone in the room can hear.
- Inflect your voice and do not stand motionless.
- Spread eye contact around audience.
- Avoid twin extremes of a fixed gaze at individuals, and never looking at anyone.
- Better to fall a little short of time allocation than run over it.
- Be selective in what you choose to present.
- Map out where you are going and summarise main points at the end.

3	
essay writing tips	

This section will show you how to:

- Quickly engage with the main arguments.
- Channel your passions constructively.
- Note your main arguments in an outline.
- Find and focus on your central topic questions.
- Weave quotations into your essay.

Getting into the flow

In essay writing one of your first aims should be to get your mind active and engaged with your subject. Tennis players like to go out on to the court and hit the ball back and forth just before the competitive match begins. This allows them to judge the bounce of the ball, feel its weight against their racket, get used to the height of the net, the parameters of the court and other factors such as temperature, light, sun and the crowd. In the same way you can 'warm up' for your essay by tossing the ideas to and fro within your head before you begin to write. This will allow you to think within the framework of your topic, and this will be especially important if you are coming to the subject for the first time.

The tributary principle

A tributary is a stream that runs into a main river as it wends its way to the sea. Similarly in an essay you should ensure that every idea you introduce is moving toward the overall theme you are addressing. Your idea might of course be relevant to a subheading that is in turn relevant to a main heading. Every idea you introduce is to be a 'feeder' into the flowing theme. In addition to tributaries, there can also be 'distributaries', which are streams that flow away from the river. In an essay these would represent the ideas that run away from the main stream of thought and leave the reader trying to work out what their relevance may have been. It is one thing to have grasped your subject thoroughly, but quite another to convince your reader that this is the case. Your aim should be to build up ideas sentence-by-sentence and paragraph-by-paragraph, until you have communicated your clear purpose to the reader.

It is important in essay writing that you not only include material that is relevant, but that you also make the linking statements that show the connection to the reader.

Listing and linking the key concepts

All subjects will have central concepts that can sometimes be usefully labelled by a single word. Course textbooks may include a glossary of terms and these provide a direct route to the beginning of efficient mastery of the topic. The central words or terms are the essential raw materials that you will need to build upon. Ensure that you learn the words and their definitions, and that you can go on to link the key words together so that in your learning activities you will add understanding to your basic memory work.

It is useful to list your key words under general headings if that is possible and logical. You may not always see the connections immediately but when you later come back to a problem that seemed intractable, you will often find that your thinking is much clearer.

EXAMPLE   Write an essay on 'Aspects and perceptions of consumer behaviour'.

You might decide to draft your outline points in the following manner (or you may prefer to use a mind map approach):

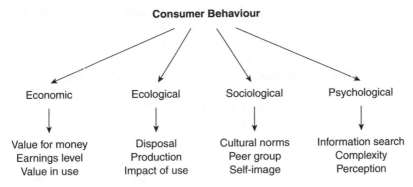

Figure 3.1   Mind map

An adversarial system

In higher education students are required to make the transition from descriptive to critical writing. If you can think of the critical approach like a law case that is being conducted where there is both a prosecution and a defence, your concern should be for objectivity, transparency and fairness. No matter how passionately you may feel about a given cause you must not allow information to be filtered out because of your personal prejudice. An essay is not to become a crusade for a cause in which the contrary arguments are not addressed in an even-handed manner. This means that you should show awareness that opposite views are held and you should at least represent these as accurately as possible.

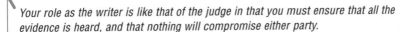

Your role as the writer is like that of the judge in that you must ensure that all the evidence is heard, and that nothing will compromise either party.

Stirring up passions

The above points do not of course mean that you are not entitled to a personal persuasion or to feel passionately about your subject. On the contrary such feelings may well be a marked advantage if you can bring them under control and channel them into balanced, effective writing (see example below). Some students may be struggling at the other end of the spectrum – being required to write about a topic that they feel quite indifferent about. As you engage with your topic and toss the ideas around in your mind, you will hopefully find that your interest is stimulated, if only at an intellectual level initially. How strongly you feel about a topic, or how much you are interested in it, may depend on whether you choose the topic yourself or whether it has been given to you as an obligatory assignment.

> *It is important that in a large project (such as a dissertation) you choose a topic for which you can maintain your motivation, momentum and enthusiasm.*

EXAMPLE **An issue that may stir up passions: arguments for and against societal marketing**

For

- Business has a responsibility to society at large.
- People are increasingly critical of firms which do not take responsibility for their action.
- Employees prefer to work for a responsible firm.
- Some shareholders will not invest in irresponsible firms.
- The law does not always protect the most vulnerable people.

Against

- A company's first responsibility is to its shareholders and employees.
- It is impossible to run a business in a way that does not cause harm to somebody.
- Companies are not qualified to judge the end results of their actions.
- There is considerable disagreement about what constitutes damaging actions.
- Governments are in the best position to regulate firms.
- One firm acting alone will lose out to unscrupulous firms.

Structuring an outline

Whenever you sense a flow of inspiration to write on a given subject, it is essential that you put this into a structure that will allow your inspiration to be communicated clearly. It is a basic principle in all walks of life that structure and order facilitate good communication. Therefore, when you have the flow of inspiration in your essay you must get this into a structure that will allow the marker to recognise the true quality of your work. For example you might plan for an introduction, conclusion, three main headings and each of these with several subheadings (see example below). Moreover, you may decide not to include your headings in your final presentation – namely just use them initially to structure and balance your arguments. Once you have drafted this outline you can then easily sketch an introduction, and you will be well prepared for the conclusion when you arrive at that point.

> *A good structure will help you to balance the weight of each of your arguments against each other, and arrange your points in the order that will facilitate the fluent progression of your argument.*

EXAMPLE   **Write an essay that assesses the dynamics of the housing market in the decision to purchase or delay.**

1   The quest to be on the property ladder

   (a)   A house is an investment.
   (b)   Rent payments are a 'black hole' for money.
   (c)   Insufficient quantity of houses for growing needs.
   (d)   Social pressure to be a homeowner.

2   Compounded problems for first time buyers

   (a)   Delay in purchase to save deposit.
   (b)   Ratio balance of salary against mortgage.
   (c)   Balancing mortgage costs with preferred lifestyle.
   (d)   Balancing the choice of house with the choice of area.

3   The problem of inflationary pressures

   (a)   Uncertainty of interest rates and world economies.
   (b)   Income may fall behind inflation.
   (c)   Future house price slumps could create negative equity.
   (d)   Conflicting reports in economic forecasts.

Finding major questions

When you are constructing a draft outline for an essay or project, you should ask what is the major question or questions you wish to address.

It would be useful to make a list of all the issues that spring to mind that you might wish to tackle. The ability to design a good question is an art form that should be cultivated, and such questions will allow you to impress your assessor with the quality of your thinking.

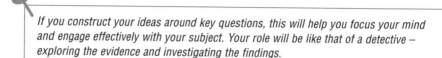

If you construct your ideas around key questions, this will help you focus your mind and engage effectively with your subject. Your role will be like that of a detective – exploring the evidence and investigating the findings.

To illustrate the point, consider the example presented below. If you were asked to write an essay about the effectiveness of advertising on television you might as your starting point pose the following questions.

EXAMPLE   **The effectiveness of advertising on television: initial questions.**

- Are the advertisements interesting and engaging?
- Are they repeated enough so that people have the opportunity to take in the information?
- Are the advertisements designed in an appropriate way?
- Do people stay in the room when the advertisements are shown?
- If they do stay in the room, do they actually watch the advertisements?
- Do the advertisements generate an adequate response rate?
- What systems do we have for assessing the effectiveness of the advertisements?
- What are the advertisements intended to achieve?

Rest your case

It should be your aim to give the clear impression that your arguments are not based entirely on hunches, bias, feelings or intuition. In exams and essay questions it is usually assumed (even if not directly specified) that you will appeal to evidence to support your claims. Therefore, when you write your essay you should ensure that it is liberally sprinkled with citations and evidence. By the time the assessor reaches the end of your work, he or she should be convinced that your conclusions are evidence based. A fatal flaw to be avoided is to make claims for which you have provided no authoritative source.

> *Give the clear impression that what you have asserted is derived from recognised sources (including up-to-date sources). It also looks impressive if you spread your citations across your essay rather than compressing them into a paragraph or two at the beginning and end.*

Some examples of how you might introduce your evidence and sources are provided below:

According to O'Neil (1999) ...
Wilson (2003) has concluded that ...
Taylor (2004) found that ...
It has been claimed by McKibben (2002) that ...
Appleby (2001) asserted that ...
A review of the evidence by Lawlor (2004) suggests that ...
Findings from a meta-analysis presented by Rea (2003) would indicate that ...

It is sensible to vary the expression used so that you are not monotonous and repetitive, and it also aids variety to introduce researchers' names at various places in the sentence (not always at the beginning). It is advisable to choose the expression that is most appropriate – for example you can make a stronger statement about reviews that have identified recurrent and predominant trends in findings as opposed to one study that appears to run contrary to all the rest.

> *Credit is given for the use of caution and discretion when this is clearly needed.*

Careful use of quotations

Although it is desirable to present a good range of cited sources, it is not judicious to present these as 'patchwork quilt' – namely you just paste together what others have said with little thought for interpretative comment or coherent structure. It is a good general point to aim to avoid very lengthy quotes – short ones can be very effective. Aim at blending the quotations as naturally as possible into the flow of your sentences. Also it is good to vary your practices – sometimes use short, direct, brief quotes (cite page number as well as author and year), and at times you can summarise the gist of a quote in your own words. In this case you should cite the author's name and year of publication but leave out quotation marks and page number.

Use your quotes and evidence in a manner that demonstrates that you have thought the issues through, and have integrated them in a manner that shows you have been focused and selective in the use of your sources.

In terms of referencing, practice may vary from one discipline to the next, but some general points that will go a long way in contributing to good practice are:

- If a reference is cited in the text, it must be in the list at the end (and vice-versa).
- Names and dates in text should correspond exactly with list in references or bibliography.
- List of references and bibliography should be in alphabetical order by the surname (not the initials) of the author or first author.
- Any reference you make in the text should be traceable by the reader (they should clearly be able to identify and trace the source).

A clearly defined introduction

In an introduction to an essay you have the opportunity to define the problem or issue that is being addressed and to set it within context. Resist the temptation to elaborate on any issue at the introductory stage. For example, think of a composer who throws out hints and suggestions of the motifs that the orchestra will later develop. What he or she does in the introduction is to provide little tasters of what will follow in order to whet the audience's appetite. If you go back to the analogy of the game of tennis, you can think of the introduction as marking out the boundaries of the court in which the game is to be played.

If you leave the introduction and definition of your problem until the end of your writing, you will be better placed to map out the directions that will be taken.

An example for practice, if you wish, can be engaged if you look back at the drafted outline on assessing the dynamics of the housing market. Try to design an introduction for that essay in about three or four sentences.

Conclusion – adding the finishing touches

In the conclusion you should aim to tie your essay together in a clear and coherent manner. It is your last chance to leave an overall impression in your reader's mind. Therefore, you will at this stage want to do justice to your efforts and not sell yourself short. This is your opportunity to identify where the strongest evidence points or where the balance of probability lies. The conclusion to an exam question often has to be written hurriedly under the pressure of time, but with an essay (coursework) you have time to reflect on, refine and adjust the content to your satisfaction. It should be your goal to make the conclusion a smooth finish that does justice to the range of content in summary and succinct form. Do not underestimate the value of an effective conclusion. 'Sign off' your essay in a manner that brings closure to the treatment of your subject.

The conclusion facilitates the chance to demonstrate where the findings have brought us to date, to highlight the issues that remain unresolved and to point to where future research should take us.

Top-down and bottom-up clarity

A word processor gives you the opportunity to refine each sentence and paragraph of your essay. Each sentence is like a tributary that leads into the stream of the paragraph that in turn leads into the mainstream of the essay. From a 'top-down' perspective (namely starting at the top with your major outline points), clarity is facilitated by the structure you draft in your outline. You can ensure that the subheadings are appropriately placed under the most relevant main heading, and that both sub and main headings are arranged in logical sequence. From a 'bottom-up' perspective (namely building up the details that 'flesh out' your main points), you should check that each sentence is a 'feeder' for the predominant concept in a given paragraph. When all this is done you can check that the transition from one point to the next is smooth rather than abrupt.

Checklist – summary for essay writing:

✓ Before you start – have a 'warm up' by tossing the issues around in your head.
✓ List the major concepts and link them in fluent form.
✓ Design a structure (outline) that will facilitate balance, progression, fluency and clarity.
✓ Pose questions and address these in critical fashion.
✓ Demonstrate that your arguments rest on evidence and spread cited sources across your essay.
✓ Provide an introduction that sets the scene and a conclusion that rounds off the arguments.

EXERCISE

Attempt to write (or at least think about) some additional features that would help facilitate good essay writing.

✓ ....

✓ ....

✓ ....

✓ ....

✓ ....

In the above checklist you could have features such as originality, clarity in sentence and paragraph structure, applied aspects, addressing a subject you feel passionately about and the ability to avoid going off on a tangent.

4	
revision hints and tips	

This section will show you how to:

➢ Map out your accumulated material for revision.
➢ Choose summary tags to guide your revision.
➢ Keep well organised folders for revision.
➢ Make use of effective memory techniques.
➢ Revise combining bullet points and in-depth reading.
➢ Profit from the benefits of revising with others.
➢ Attend to the practical exam details that will help keep panic at bay.
➢ Use strategies that keep you task-focused during the exam.
➢ Select and apply relevant points from your prepared outlines.

The return journey

In a return journey you will usually pass by all the same places that you had already passed when you were outward bound. If you had observed the various landmarks on your outward journey you would be likely to remember them on your return. Similarly, revision is a means to 'revisit' what you have encountered before. Familiarity with your material can help reduce anxiety, inspire confidence and fuel motivation for further learning and good performance.

If you are to capitalise on your revision period, then you must have your materials arranged and at hand for the time when you are ready to make your 'return journey' through your notes.

Start at the beginning

A strategy for revision should be on your mind from your first lecture at the beginning of your academic semester. You should be like the squirrel that stores up nuts for the winter. Do not waste any lecture, tutorial, seminar, group discussion, and so on by letting the material evaporate into thin air. Get into the habit of making a few guidelines for revision after each learning activity. Keep a folder, or file, or little notebook that is reserved for revision and write out the major points that you have learnt. By establishing this regular practice you will find that what you have learnt becomes consolidated in your mind, and you will also be in a better position to 'import' and 'export' your material both within and across subjects.

If you do this regularly, and do not make the task too tedious, you will be amazed at how much useful summary material you have accumulated when revision time comes.

Compile summary notes

It would be useful and convenient to have a little notebook or cards on which you can write outline summaries that provide you with an overview of your subject at a glance. You could also use treasury tags to hold different batches of cards together whilst still allowing for inserts and re-sorting. Such practical resources can easily be slipped into your pocket or bag and produced when you are on the bus or train or whilst sitting in a traffic jam. They would also be useful if you are standing in a queue or waiting for someone who is not in a rush! A glance over your notes will consolidate your learning and will also activate your mind to think further about your subject. Therefore it would also be useful to make note of the questions that you would like to think about in greater depth. Your primary task is to get into the habit of constructing outline notes that will be useful for revision, and a worked example is provided below.

There is a part of the mind that will continue to work on problems when you have moved on to focus on other issues. Therefore, if you feed on useful, targeted information, your mind will continue to work on 'automatic pilot' after you have 'switched off'.

EXAMPLE   **Part of a course on marketing communication is the use of non-verbal communication, and your outline revision structure for this might be as follows.**

1   Aspects of non-verbal communication that run parallel with language:

- Pauses.
- Tone of voice.
- Inflection of voice.
- Speed of voice.

2   Facets of non-verbal communication related to use of body parts:

- How close to stand to others.
- How much to use the hands.
- Whether to make physical contact – for example, touching, hugging, handshake.
- Extent and frequency of eye contact.

3   General features that augment communication:

- Use of smiles and frowns.
- Use of eyebrows.
- Expressions of boredom or interest.
- Dress and appearance.

Keep organised records

People who have a fulfilled career have usually developed the twin skills of time and task management. It is worth pausing to remember that you can use your academic training to prepare for your future career in this respect. Therefore, ensure that you do not fall short of your potential because these qualities have not been cultivated. One important tactic is to keep a folder for each subject and divide this topic-by-topic. You can keep your topics in the same order in which they are presented in your course lectures. Bind them together in a ring binder or folder and use subject dividers to keep them apart. Make a numbered list of the contents at the beginning of the folder, and list each topic clearly as it marks a new section in your folder. Another important practice is to place all your notes on a given topic within the appropriate section. Don't put off this simple task. Do it straight away. Notes may come from lectures, seminars, tutorials, Internet searches, personal notes, and so on. It is also essential that when you remove these for consultation that you return them to their 'home' immediately after use.

Academic success has as much to do with good organisation and planning, as it has to do with ability. The value of the quality material you have accumulated on your academic programme may be diminished because you have not organised it into an easily retrievable form.

EXAMPLE Fun example of an organised record – a history of romantic relationships.

- Physical features my girlfriends/boyfriends have shared or differed in.
- Common and diverse personality characteristics.
- Shared and contrasting interests.
- Frequency of dates with each.
- Places frequented together.
- Contact with both circles of friends.
- Use of humour in our communication.
- Frequency and resolution of conflicts.
- Mutual generosity.
- Courtesy and consideration.
- Punctuality.
- Dress and appearance.

Let's imagine that you had five girlfriends/boyfriends over the last few years. Each of the five names could be included under all of the above subjects. You could then compare them with each other – looking at what they had in common and how they differed. Moreover, you could think of the ones you liked best and least, and then look through your dossier to establish why this might have been. You could also judge who had most and least in common with you and whether you were more attracted to those who differed most from you. The questions open to you can go on and on. The real point here is that you will have gathered a wide variety of material that is organised in such a way that will allow you to use a range of evidence to come up with some satisfactory and authoritative conclusions – if that is possible in matters so directly related to the heart!

Use past papers

Revision will be very limited if it is confined to memory work. You should by all means read over your revision cards or notebook and keep the picture of the major facts in front of your mind's eye. It is also, however, essential that you become familiar with previous exam papers so that you will have some idea of how the questions are likely to be framed. Therefore, build up a good range of past exam papers (especially recent ones) and add these to your folder. When cows and sheep have grazed, they lie down and 'chew the cud'. That is, they regurgitate what they have eaten and take time to digest the food thoroughly.

> *If you think over previous exam questions, this will help you not only recall what you have deposited in your memory, but also to develop your understanding of the issues. The questions from past exam papers, and further questions that you have developed yourself, will allow you to 'chew the cud'.*

WORKED EXAMPLE   **Evaluate the pleasures and problems of keeping a pet.**

Immediately you can see that you will require two lists and you can begin to work on documenting your reasons under each as below:

Problems

- Vet and food bills.
- Restrictions on holidays/weekends away.
- Friends may not visit.
- Allergies.
- Smells and cleanliness.
- Worries about leaving pet alone.

Pleasures

- Companionship.
- Fun and relaxation.
- Satisfaction from caring.
- Cuddles.
- Contact with other pet owners.
- Good distraction from problems.

You will have also noticed that the word 'evaluate' is in the question – so your mind must go to work on making judgements. You may decide to work through problems first and then through pleasures, or it may be your preference to compare point by point as you go along. Whatever conclusion you come to may be down to personal subjective preference but at least you will have worked through all the issues from both stand-points. The lesson is to ensure that part of your revision should include critical thinking as well as memory work.

You cannot think adequately without the raw materials provided by your memory deposits.

Employ effective mnemonics (memory aids)

The Greek word from which 'mnemonics' is derived refers to a tomb – a structure that is built in memory of a loved one, friend or respected person. 'Mnemonics' can be simply defined as aids to memory – devices that will help you recall information that might otherwise be difficult to retrieve from memory. For example, if you find an old toy in the attic of your house, it may suddenly trigger a flood of childhood memories associated with it. Mnemonics can therefore be thoughts of as keys that open memory's storehouse.

Visualisation is one technique that can be used to aid memory. For example, the location method is where a familiar journey is visualised and you can 'place' the facts that you wish to remember at various land-marks along the journey – for example, a bus stop, a car park, a shop, a store, a bend, a police station, a traffic light, and so on. This has the advantage of making an association of the information you have to learn with other material that is already firmly embedded and structured in your memory. Therefore, once the relevant memory is activated, a dynamic 'domino effect' will be triggered. However, there is no reason why you cannot use a whole toolkit of mnemonics. Some examples and illustrations of these are presented below.

1   *If you can arrange your subject matter in a logical sequence this will ensure that your series of facts will also connect with each other and one will trigger the other in recall.*
2   *You can use memory devices either at the stage of initial learning or when you later return to consolidate.*

Location method

Defined above.

Visualisation

Turn information into pictures – for example, the example given about the problems and pleasures of pets could be envisaged as two tug-of-war teams that pull against each other. You could visualise each player as an argument and have the label written on his or her T-shirt. The war could start with two players and then be joined by another two and so on. In addition you could compare each player's weight to the strength of each argument. You might also want to make use of colour – your favourite colour for the winning team and the colour you dislike most for the losers!

Alliteration's artful aid

Find a series of words that all begin with the same letter. See the example below related to the experiments of Ebbinghaus.

Peg system

'Hang' information on to a term so that when you hear the term you will remember the ideas connected with it (an umbrella term). In the example on consumer behaviour there were four different types – economic, ecological, sociological and psychological. Under economic you could remember value for money, earnings level, and value in use.

Hierarchical system

This is a development of the previous point with higher order, middle order and lower order terms. For example you could think of the continents of the world (higher order), and then group these into the countries under them (middle order). Under countries you could have cities, rivers and mountains (lower order).

Acronyms

Take the first letter of all the key words and make a word from these. An example from marketing strategy is SWOT – Strengths, Weaknesses, Opportunities and Threats.

Mind maps

These have become very popular – they allow you to draw lines that stretch out from the central idea and to develop the subsidiary ideas in the same way. It is a little like the pegging and hierarchical methods combined and turned sideways! This method has the advantage of giving you the complete picture at a glance, although they can become a complex work of art!

Rhymes and chimes

Words that rhyme and words that end with a similar sound (for example, commemoration, celebration, anticipation). These provide another dimension to memory work by including sound. Memory can be enhanced when information is processed in various modalities – for example, hearing, seeing, speaking, visualising.

A confidence booster

At the end of the nineteenth century, Ebbinghaus and his assistant memorised lists of nonsense words (could not be remembered by being attached to meaning), and then endeavoured to recall these. What they discovered was:

- Some words could be recalled freely from memory while others appeared to be forgotten.
- Words that could not be recalled were later recognised as belonging to the lists (namely were not new additions).
- When the lists were jumbled into a different sequence, the experimenters were able to re-jumble them into the original sequence.
- When the words that were 'forgotten' were learnt again, the learning process was much easier the second time (namely there was evidence of re-learning savings).

The four points of this experiment can be remembered by alliteration: Recall, Recognition, Reconstruction and Re-learning savings. This experiment has been described as a confidence booster because it demonstrates that memory is more powerful than is often imagined, especially when we consider that Ebbinghaus and his assistant did not have the advantage of processing the meaning of the words.

Alternate between methods

It is not sufficient to present outline points in response to an exam question (although it is better to do this than do nothing if you have run out of time in your exam). Your aim should be to put 'meat on the bones' by adding substance, evidence and arguments to your basic points. You should work at finding the balance between the two methods – outline revision cards might be best reserved for short bus journeys, whereas extended reading might be better employed for longer revision slots at home or in the library. Your ultimate goal should be to bring together an effective working approach that will enable you to face your exam questions comprehensively and confidently.

In revision it is useful to alternate between scanning over your outline points, and reading through your notes, articles, chapters, and so on in an in-depth manner. Also, the use of different times, places and methods will provide you with the variety that might prevent monotony and facilitate freshness.

WORKED EXAMPLE   Imagine that you are doing a course on the human body.

Your major outline topics might be:

- Names, positions and purpose of bones in the body.
- Names and position of organs in the body.
- The organs and chemicals associated with digestion.
- Composition, function and routes of blood.
- Parts and processes of the body associated with breathing.
- Components and dynamics of the nervous and lymphatic systems.

- Structure, nature and purpose of the skin.
- Role of the brain in controlling and mediating the above systems.

This outline would be your overall, bird's eye view of the course. You could then choose one of the topics and have all your key terms under that. For example, under digestion you might have listed: mouth, oesophagus, stomach, duodenum, intestine, liver, vagus nerve, hypothalamus, hydrochloric acid and carbohydrates. In order to move from memory to understanding you would need to consider the journey of food through the human digestive system.

If you alternate between memory work and reading, you will soon be able to think through the processes by just looking at your outlines.

Revising with others

If you can find a few other students to revise with, this will provide another fresh approach to the last stages of your learning. First ensure that others carry their workload and are not merely using the hard work of others as a short cut to success. Of course you should think of group sessions as one of the strings on your violin, but not the only string. This collective approach would allow you to assess your strengths and weaknesses (showing you where you are off track), and to benefit from the resources and insights of others. Before you meet up you can each design some questions for the whole group to address. The group could also go through past exam papers and discuss the points that might provide an effective response to each question. It should not be the aim of the group to provide standard and identical answers for each group member to mimic. Group work is currently deemed to be advantageous by educationalists, and team work is held to be a desirable employability quality.

Each individual should aim to use their own style and content whilst drawing on and benefiting from the group's resources.

EXERCISE

Make a list of the advantages and disadvantages of revising in small groups.

Advantages	Disadvatages
1	....
2	....
3	....
4	....
5	....

Can the disadvantages be eliminated or at least minimised?

Checklist – good study habits for revision time:

✓ Set a date for the 'official' beginning of revision and prepare for 'revision mode'.
✓ Do not force cramming by leaving revision too late.
✓ Take breaks from revision to avoid saturation.
✓ Indulge in relaxing activities to give your mind a break from pressure.
✓ Minimise or eliminate use of alcohol during the revision season.
✓ Get into a good rhythm of sleep to allow renewal of your mind.
✓ Avoid excessive caffeine especially at night so that sleep is not disrupted.
✓ Try to adhere to regular eating patterns.
✓ Try to have a brisk walk in fresh air each day (for example, in the park).
✓ Avoid excessive dependence on junk food and snacks.

EXERCISE

Write your own checklist on what you add to the revision process to ensure it was not just a memory exercise.

✓ ....

✓ ....

✓ ....

✓ ....

✓ ....

In the above exercise, what you could add to memory work during revision might include using past exam papers, setting problem-solving tasks, doing drawings to show connections and directions between various concepts, explaining concepts to student friends in joint revision sessions, devising your own mock exam questions.

5	
exam hints and tips	

This section will show you how to:

➢ Develop strategies for controlling your nervous energy.
➢ Tackle worked examples of time and task management in exams.
➢ Attend to the practical details associated with the exam.
➢ Stay focused on the exam questions.
➢ Link revision outlines to strategy for addressing exam questions.

Handling your nerves

Exam nerves are not unusual and it has been concluded that test anxiety arises because of the perception that your performance is being evaluated, that the consequences are likely to be serious and that you are working under the pressure of a time restriction. However, it has also been asserted that the activation of the autonomic nervous system is adaptive in that it is designed to prompt us to take action in order to avoid danger. If you focus on the task at hand rather than on feeding a downward negative spiral in your thinking patterns, this will help you keep your nerves under control.

In the run up to your exams you can practise some simple relaxation techniques that will help you bring stress under control.

> It is a very good thing if you can interpret your nervous reactions positively, but the symptoms are more likely to be problematic if you interpret them negatively, pay too much attention to them or allow them to interfere with your exam preparation or performance.

Practices that may help reduce or buffer the effects of exam stress

- Listening to music.
- Going for a brisk walk.
- Simple breathing exercises.
- Some muscle relaxation.
- Watching a movie.
- Enjoying some laughter.
- Doing some exercise.
- Relaxing in a bath (with music if preferred).

The best choice is going to be the one (or combination) that works best for you – perhaps to be discovered by trial and error. Some of the above techniques can be practised on the morning of the exam, and even the memory of them can be used just before the exam. For example, you could run over a relaxing tune in your head, and have this echo inside you as you enter the exam room. The idea behind all this is, first, stress levels must come down, and second, relaxing thoughts will serve to displace stressful reactions. It has been said that stress is the body's call to take action, but anxiety is a maladaptive response to that call.

> It is important you are convinced that your stress levels can come under control, and that you can have a say in this. Do not give anxiety a vacuum to work in.

Time management with examples

The all-important matter as you approach an exam is to develop the belief that you can take control of the situation. As you work through the list of issues that you need to address, you will be able to tick them off one by one. One of the issues you will need to be clear about before the exam is the length of time you should allocate to each question. Sometimes this can be quite simple (although it is always necessary to read the rubric carefully) – for example, if two questions are to be answered in a two-hour paper, you should allow one hour for each question. If it is a two-hour paper with one essay question and five shorter questions, you could allow one hour for the essay and 12 minutes each for the shorter questions. However, you always need to check out the weighting for the marks on each question, and you will also need to deduct whatever time it takes you to read over the paper and to choose your questions. See if you can work out a time management strategy in each of the following scenarios. More importantly, give yourself some practice on the papers you are likely to face.

Remember to check if the structure of your exam paper is the same as in previous years, and do not forget that excessive time on your 'strongest' question may not compensate for very poor answers to other questions. Also ensure that you read the rubric carefully in the exam.

EXERCISE

Examples for working out the division of exam labour by time:

1 A three-hour paper with four compulsory questions (equally weighted in marks).

2 A three-hour paper with two essays and ten short questions (each of the three sections carry one-third of the marks).

3 A two-hour paper with two essay questions and 100 multiple-choice questions (half marks are on the two essays and half marks on the multiple choice section).

Get into the calculating frame of mind and be sure to have the calculations done before the exam. Ensure that the structure of the exam has not changed since the last one. Also deduct the time taken to read over the paper in allocating time to each question.

Suggested answers to previous exercise

1 This allows 45 minutes for each question (4 questions × 45 minutes = 2 hours). However, if your allow 40 minutes for each question this will give you 20 minutes (4 questions × 5 minutes) to read over the paper and plan your outlines.

2 In this example you can spend one hour on each of the two major questions, and one hour on the ten short questions. For the two major questions you could allow ten minutes for reading and planning on each, and 50 minutes for writing. In the ten short questions, you could allow six minutes in total for each (10 questions × 6 minutes = 60 minutes). However, if you allow approximately one minute reading and planning time, this will allow five minutes writing time for each question.

3 In this case you have to divide 120 minutes by three questions – this allows 40 minutes for each. You could, for example, allow five minutes reading/planning time for each essay and 35 minutes for writing (or ten minutes reading/planning and 30 minutes writing). After you have completed the two major questions you are left with 40 minutes to tackle the 100 multiple-choice questions.

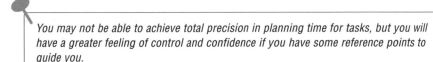

You may not be able to achieve total precision in planning time for tasks, but you will have a greater feeling of control and confidence if you have some reference points to guide you.

Task management with examples

After you have decided on the questions you wish to address, you then need to plan your answers. Some students prefer to plan all outlines and draft work at the beginning, whilst others prefer to plan and address one answer before proceeding to address the next question. Decide on your strategy before you enter the exam room and stick to your plan. When you have done your draft outline as rough work, you should allocate an appropriate time for each section. This will prevent you from excessive treatment of some aspects whilst falling short on other parts. Such careful planning will help you achieve balance, fluency and symmetry.

Keep awareness of time limitations and this will help you to write succinctly, keep focused on the task and prevent you dressing up your responses with unnecessary padding.

Some students put as much effort into their rough work as they do into their exam essay.

An over elaborate mind map may give the impression that the essay is little more than a repetition of this detailed structure, and that the quality of the content has suffered because too much time was spent on the plan.

EXERCISE

Try the following exercise.

Work within the time allocated for the following outline, allowing one hour on the question. Deduct ten minutes taken at the beginning for choice and planning.

Discuss whether it is justifiable to ban cigarette smoking in pubs and restaurants.

1   Arguments for a ban

  (a)   Health risks by sustained exposure to passive smoking.
  (b)   Employees (such as students) suffer unfairly.
  (C)   Children with parents may also be victims.

2   Arguments against a ban

  (a)   Risks may be exaggerated.
  (b)   Dangerous chemicals and pollutants in environment ignored by governments.
  (C)   Non-smokers can choose whether to frequent smoking venues.

3   Qualifying suggestions

  (a)   Better use of ventilation and extractor fans.
  (b)   Designated non-smoking areas.
  (c)   Pubs and restaurants should be addressed separately in relation to a ban.

Attend to practical details

This short section is designed to remind you of the practical details that should be attended to in preparation for an exam. There are always students who turn up late, or to the wrong venue or for the wrong exam, or do not turn up at all! Check and re-check that you have all the details of each exam correctly noted. What you don't need is to arrive late and then have to tame your panic reactions. The exam season is the time when you should aim to be at your best.

> *Turn up to the right venue in good time so that you can quieten your mind and bring your stress under control.*

Make note of the following details and check that you have taken control of each one.

Checklist – practical exam details:

- ✓ Check that you have the correct venue.
- ✓ Make sure you know how to locate the venue before the exam day.
- ✓ Ensure that the exam time you have noted is accurate.
- ✓ Allow sufficient time for your journey and consider the possibility of delays.
- ✓ Bring an adequate supply of stationery and include back up.
- ✓ Bring a watch for your time and task management.
- ✓ You may need some liquid such as a small bottle of still water.
- ✓ You may also need to bring some tissues.
- ✓ Observe whatever exam regulations your university/college has set in place.
- ✓ Fill in required personal details before the exam begins.

Control wandering thoughts

In a simple study conducted in the 1960s, Ganzer found that students who frequently lifted their heads and looked away from their scripts during exams tended to perform poorly. This makes sense because it implies that the students were taking too much time out when they should have been on task. One way to fail your exam is to get up and walk out of the test room, but another way is to 'leave' the test room mentally by being preoccupied with distracting thoughts. The distracting thoughts may be either related to the exam itself or totally irrelevant to it. The net effect of both these forms of intrusion is to distract you from the task at hand and debilitate your test performance. Read over the two lists of distracting thoughts presented below.

Typical test relevant thoughts (evaluative)

- I wish I had prepared better.
- What will the examiner think.
- Others are doing better than me.
- What I am writing is nonsense.
- Can't remember important details.

Characteristic test irrelevant thoughts (non-evaluative)

- Looking forward to this weekend?
- Which video should I watch tonight?
- His remark really annoyed me yesterday.
- Wonder how the game will go on Saturday.
- I wonder if he/she really likes me.

Research has consistently shown that distracting, intrusive thoughts during an exam are more detrimental to performance than stressful symptoms such as sweaty palms, dry mouth, tension, trembling, and so on. Moreover, it does not matter whether the distracting thoughts are negative evaluations related to the exam or are totally irrelevant to the exam. The latter may be a form of escape from the stressful situation.

Practical suggestions for controlling wandering thoughts

- Be aware that this problem is detrimental to performance.
- Do not look around to find distractions.
- If distracted, write down 'keep focused on task'.
- If distracted again, look back at above and continue to do this.
- Start to draft rough work as soon as you can.
- If you struggle with initial focus then re-read or elaborate on your rough work.
- If you have commenced your essay re-read you last paragraph (or two).
- Do not throw fuel on your distracting thoughts – starve them by re-engaging with the task at hand.

Links to revision

If you have followed the guidelines given for revision, you will be well equipped with outline plans when you enter the exam room. You may have chosen to use headings and subheadings, mind maps, hierarchical approaches or just a series of simple mnemonics. Whatever method you choose to use, you should be furnished with a series of memory triggers that will open the treasure house door for you once you begin to write.

> *Although you may have clear templates with a definite structure or framework for organising your material, you will need to be flexible about how this should be applied to your exam questions.*

For example, imagine that films are one of the topics that you will be examined on. You decide to memorise lists of films that you are familiar with under categorical headings in the following manner.

Romantic comedy	War/History/Fantasy	Space/Invasion
Notting Hill	Braveheart	Star Wars
Pretty Woman	Gladiator	Independence Day
Along came Polly	First Knight	Alien
Four Weddings and a Funeral	Troy	Men in Black

Adventure/Fantasy	Horror/Supernatural
Harry Potter	Poltergeist
Lord of the Rings	The Omen
Alice in Wonderland	Sixth Sense
Labyrinth	What Lies Beneath

The basic mental template might be these and a few other categories. You know that you will not need every last detail, although you may need to select a few from each category. For example, you might be asked to:

(a)   Compare and contrast features of comedy and horror.
(b)   Comment on films that have realistic moral lessons in them.
(c)   Discuss films that might be construed as a propaganda exercise.
(d)   Identify films where the characters are more important than the plot and vice-versa.

Some questions will put a restriction on the range of categories you can use (a), while others will allow you to dip into any category ((b), (c) and (d)). A question about fantasy would allow you scope across various categories.

> *Restrict your material to what is relevant to the question, but bear in mind that this may allow you some scope.*

Art of 'name dropping'

In most topics at university you will be required to cite studies as evidence for your arguments and to link these to the names of researchers, scholars or theorists. It will help if you can use the correct dates or at least the decades, and it is good to demonstrate that you have used contemporary sources, and have done some independent work. A marker will have dozens if not hundreds of scripts to work through and they will know if you are just repeating the same phrases from the same sources as every one else. There is inevitably a certain amount of this that must go on, but there is room for you to add fresh and original touches that demonstrate independence and imagination.

> *Give the clear impression that you have done more than the bare minimum and that you have enthusiasm for the subject. Also, spread the use of researchers' names across your exam essay rather than compressing them into, for example, the first and last paragraphs.*

Flight, fight or freeze

As previously noted, the autonomic nervous system is activated when danger or apparent danger is imminent. Of course the threat does not have to be physical, as in the case of an exam, a job interview, a driving test or a TV appearance. Indeed the ANS can be activated even at the anticipation of a future threat. However, the reaction is more likely to be stronger as you enter into the crucial time of testing or challenge. Symptoms may include deep breathing, trembling, headaches, nausea, tension, dry mouth and palpitations. How should we react to these once they have been triggered? A postman might decide to run away from a barking dog and run the risk of being chased and bitten. A second possible response is to freeze on the spot – this might arrest the animal on its tracks, but is no use in an exam situation. In contrast, to fight might not be the best strategy against the dog, but will be more productive in an exam. That is, you are going into the exam room to 'tackle' the questions, and not to run away from the challenge before you.

The final illustration below uses the analogy of archery to demonstrate how you might take control in an exam.

Lessons from archery

- ➢ Enter the exam room with a quiver full of arrows – all the points you will need to use.
- ➢ Eye up the target board you are to shoot at – choose the exam questions.
- ➢ Stand in good position for balance and vision – prepare your time management.
- ➢ Prepare your bow and arrow and take aim at the target – keep focused on the task at hand and do not be sidetracked.
- ➢ Pull the string of the bow back to get maximum thrust on the arrow – match your points to the appropriate question.
- ➢ Aim to hit the board where the best marks are (bull's eye or close) – do not be content with the minimum standard such as a mere pass.
- ➢ Pull out arrows and shoot one after another to gain maximum hits and advantage – do not be content with preparing one or two strong points.
- ➢ Make sure your arrows are sharp and the supporting bow and string are firm – choose relevant points and support with evidence.
- ➢ Avoid wasted effort by loose and careless shots – do not dress up your essay with unnecessary padding.

EXERCISE

Write your own checklist on the range of combined skills and personal qualities that you will need to be at your best in an exam.

✓ ....

✓ ....

✓ ....

✓ ....

✓ ....

With reference to the above exercise – skills might include such things as critical thinking, time and task management, focus on issues, and quick identification of problems to address. Personal qualities might include factors such as confidence, endurance, resilience, and stress control.

6	
tips on interpreting essay and exam questions	

This section will show you how to:

➢ Focus on the issues that are relevant and central.
➢ Read questions carefully and take account of all the words.
➢ Produce a balanced critique in your outline structures.
➢ Screen for the key words that will shape your response.
➢ Focus on different shades of meaning between 'critique', 'evaluate', 'discuss' and 'compare and contrast'.

What do you see?

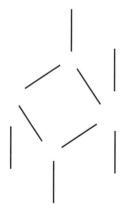

Figure 3.2   Visual illusion

The suggested explanation for visual illusions is the inappropriate use of cues – namely we try to interpret three-dimensional figures in the real world with the limitations of a two dimensional screen (the retina in the eye). We use cues such as shade, texture, size, background, and so on to interpret distance, motion, shape, and so on and we sometimes use these inappropriately. Another visual practice we engage in is to 'fill in the blanks' or join up the lines (as in the case of the nine lines above – which we might assume to be a chair). Our tendency is to impose the nearest similar and familiar template on that which we think we see. The same occurs in the social world – when we are introduced to someone of a different race we may (wrongly) assume certain things about them. The same can also apply to the way you read exam or essay questions. In these cases you are required to 'fill in the blanks' but what you fill in may be the wrong interpretation of the question. This is especially likely if you have primed yourself to expect certain questions to appear in an exam, but it can also happen in coursework essays. Although examiners do not deliberately design questions to trick you or trip you up, they cannot always prevent you from seeing things that were not designed to be there. When one student was asked what the four seasons are, the response given was, 'salt, pepper, mustard and vinegar'. This was not quite what the examiner had in mind!

> Go into the exam room, or address the coursework essay well prepared, but be flexible enough to structure your learnt material around the slant of the question.

A politician's answer

Politicians are renowned for refusing to answer questions directly or for evading them through raising other questions. A humorous example is that when a politician was asked, 'Is it true that you always answer questions by asking another?', the reply given was, 'Who told you that?' Therefore, make sure that you answer the set question, although there may be other questions that arise out of this for further study that you might want to highlight in your conclusion. As a first principle you must answer the set question and not another question that you had hoped for in the exam or essay.

> Do not leave the examiner feeling like the person who interviews a politician and goes away with the impression that the important issues have been sidestepped.

EXAMPLE Discuss the strategies for improving the sale of fresh fruit and vegetables in the market place at the point of delivery to the customer.

Directly relevant points

- Stall and fruit kept clean.
- Well presented/arranged produce.
- Use of colour and variety.
- Position of stall in market (for example, smells).
- Use of free samples.
- Appearance and manner of assistants.
- Competitive prices.

Less relevant points

- Advantages of organic growth.
- Arguments for vegetarianism.
- Cheaper transport for produce.
- Value of locally grown produce.
- Strategies for pest control in growth.
- Arguments for refrigeration in transit.
- Cheaper rents for markets.

Although some of the points listed in the second column may be relevant to sales overall, they are not as directly relevant to sales 'in the market place at the point of delivery to the customer'. If the question had included the quality of the produce then some of those issues should be addressed. Also it could be argued that some of these issues could be highlighted on a board at the stall – for example, 'Only organically grown produce is sold at this stall'. So some of the points could be mentioned briefly in this way without going off on a tangent.

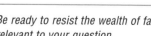

> Be ready to resist the wealth of fascinating material at your disposal that is not directly relevant to your question.

Missing your question

A student bitterly complained after an exam that the topic he had revised so thoroughly had not been tested in the exam. The first response to that is that students should always cover enough topics to avoid selling themselves short in the exam – the habit of 'question spotting' is always a risky game to play. However, the reality in the anecdotal example was that the question the student was looking for was there, but he had not seen it. He had expected the question to be couched in certain words and he could not find these when he scanned over the questions in blind panic. Therefore, the simple lesson is always read over the questions carefully, slowly and thoughtfully. This practice is time well spent.

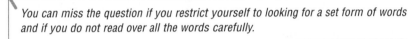

You can miss the question if you restrict yourself to looking for a set form of words and if you do not read over all the words carefully.

Write it down

If you write down the question you have chosen to address, and perhaps quietly articulate it with your lips, you are more likely to process fully its true meaning and intent. Think of how easy it is to misunderstand a question that had been put to you verbally because you have misinterpreted the tone or emphasis.

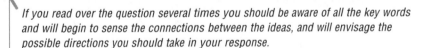

If you read over the question several times you should be aware of all the key words and will begin to sense the connections between the ideas, and will envisage the possible directions you should take in your response.

Take the following humorous example:

(a)   What is that on the road ahead?
(b)   What is that on the road, a head?

Question (a) calls for the identification of an object (what is that?), but question (b) has converted this into an object that suggests there has been a decapitation! Ensure therefore that you understand the direction the question is pointing you towards so that you do not go off at a tangent. One word in the question that is not properly attended to can throw you completely off track as in the following example:

(a) Discuss whether the love of money is the root of all evil.
(b) Discuss whether money is the root of all evil.

These are two completely different questions as (a) suggests that the real problem with money is inherent in faulty human use – that is, money itself may not be a bad thing if it is used as a servant and not a master. Whereas (b) may suggest that behind every evil act that has ever been committed money is likely to have been implicated somewhere in the motive.

Pursue a critical approach

In degree courses you are usually expected to write critically rather than merely descriptively, although it may be necessary to use some minimal descriptive substance as the raw material for your debate.

EXAMPLE   Evaluate the evidence whether the American astronauts really walked on the moon, or whether this was a stage-managed hoax in a studio.

Arguments for studio

- Flag blowing on moon?
- Explain the shadows.
- Why no stars seen?
- Why little dust blowing at landing?
- Can humans survive passing through the radiation belt?

Arguments for walking

- Communicates with laser reflectors left on moon.
- Retrieved rocks show patterns that are not earthly.
- How could such a hoax be protected?
- American activities were monitored by Soviets.
- Plausible explanations for arguments against walking.

Given that the question is about a critical evaluation of the evidence, you would need to address the issues one by one from both standpoints. What you should not do is digress into a tangent about the physical characteristics of the Beagle space ship or the astronauts' suits. Neither should you be drawn into a lengthy description of lunar features and contours even if you have in-depth knowledge of these.

Analyse the parts

In an effective sports team the end product is always greater than the sum of the parts. Similarly, a good essay cannot be constructed without reference to the parts. Furthermore, the parts will arise as you break down the question into the components it suggests to you. Although the breaking down of a question into components is not sufficient for an excellent essay, it is a necessary starting point.

> To achieve a good response to an exam or essay question, aim to integrate all the individual issues presented in a manner that gives shape and direction to your efforts.

EXAMPLE 1   Discuss whether the design and execution of press advertising affects message retention by consumers.

Two parts to this question are clearly suggested – design and execution, and you would need to do justice to each in your answer. Other issues that arise in relation to these are left for you to suggest and discuss. Examples might be perception, customer centrality, media buying, or brand perceptions.

EXAMPLE 2   Evaluate the advantages and disadvantages of giving students course credit for participation in experiments.

This is a straightforward question in that you have two major sections – advantages and disadvantages. You are left with the choice of the issues that you wish to address, and you can arrange these in the order you prefer. Your aim should be to ensure that you do not have a lopsided view of this even if you feel quite strongly one way or the other.

EXAMPLE 3   Trace in a critical manner Western society's changing attitudes to the globalisation of markets.

In this case you might want to consider the role of governments, major corporations, consumers, and the media. However, you will need to have some reference points to the past as you are asked to address the issue of change. There would also be scope to look at where the strongest influences for globalisation arise and where the strongest resistance comes from. You might argue that the changes have been dramatic or evolutionary.

Give yourself plenty of practice at thinking of questions in this kind of way – both with topics on and not on your course. Topics not on your course that really interest you may be a helpful way to 'break you in' to this critical way of thinking.

Luchins and learning sets

In a series of experiments, Luchins allowed children to learn how to solve a problem that involved pouring water from and into a series of jugs of various sizes and shapes. He then gave them other problems that could be solved by following the same sequence. However, when he later gave them another problem that could be solved through a simpler sequence, they went about solving it through the previously learnt procedure. In this case the original approach was more difficult but it had become so set in the children's minds that they were blinded to the shorter, more direct route.

EXAMPLE   How much did the wealthy Scottish man leave behind?

The story is told of a wealthy Scottish man who died, and no one in his village knew how much he had left behind. The issue was debated and gossiped about for some time, but one man claimed that he knew how much the man had left. He teased all the debaters and gossips in the village night after night. Eventually he let his big secret out, and the answer was that the rich man had left 'all of it' behind! No one in the village had been able to work out the mischievous man's little ruse because of the convergent thinking style they used. Some exam questions may require you to be divergent in the way you think (namely, not just one obvious solution to the problem). This may mean being like a detective in the way you investigate and problem solve. The only difference is that you may need to set up the problem as well as the solution!

Get into the habit of 'stepping sideways' and looking at questions from several angles. The best way to do this is by practice, for example, on previous exam papers.

Checklist – ensuring that questions are understood before being fully addressed:

✓ Read over the chosen question several times.
✓ Write it down to ensure that it is clear.
✓ Check that you have not omitted any important aspect or point of emphasis.
✓ Ensure that you do not wrongly impose preconceived expectations on the question.
✓ Break the question into parts (dismantle and rebuild).

EXERCISE

Write your own checklist on any additional points of guidance for exams that you have picked up from tutors or textbooks.

✓ ....

✓ ....

✓ ....

✓ ....

✓ ....

When asked to discuss

Students often ask how much of their own opinion they should include in an essay. In a discussion, when you raise one issue, another one can arise out of it. One tutor used to introduce his lectures by saying that he was going to 'unpack' the arguments. When you unpack an object (such as a new desk that has to be assembled), you first remove the overall packaging, such as a large box, and then proceed to remove the covers from all the component parts. After that you attempt to assemble all the parts, according to the given design, so that they hold together in the intended manner. In a discussion your aim should be not just to identify and define all the parts that contribute, but also to show where they fit (or don't fit) into the overall picture.

Although the word 'discuss' implies some allowance for your opinion, remember that this should be informed opinion rather than groundless speculation. Also, there must be direction, order, structure and end project.

Checklist – features of a response to a 'discuss' question:

✓ Contains a chain of issues that lead into each other in sequence.
✓ Clear shape and direction is unfolded in the progression of the argument.
✓ Underpinned by reference to findings and certainties.
✓ Identification of issues where doubt remains.
✓ Tone of argument may be tentative but should not be vague.

If a critique is requested

One example that might help clarify what is involved in a critique is the hotly debated topic of whether marketing's role is to make selling obsolete. It would be important in the interest of balance and fairness to present all sides and shades of the argument. You would then look at whether there is available evidence to support each argument, and you might introduce issues that have been coloured by prejudice, tradition, religion and legislation. It would be an aim to identify emotional arguments, arguments based on intuition and to get down to those arguments that really have solid evidence based support. Finally you would want to flag up where the strongest evidence appears to lie, and you should also identify issues that appear to be inconclusive. It would be expected that you should, if possible, arrive at some certainties.

EXERCISE

Write your own summary checklist for the features of a critique. You can either summarise the above points, or use your own points, or a mixture of the two.

✓ ....

✓ ....

✓ ....

✓ ....

✓ ....

If asked to compare and contrast

When asked to compare and contrast, you should be thinking in terms of similarities and differences. You should ask what the two issues share in common, and what features of each are distinct. Your preferred strategy for tackling this might be to work first through all the similarities and then through all the contrasts (or vice versa). Conversely, through a similarity and contrast, followed by another similarity and contrast and so on.

EXAMPLE   Compare and contrast the uses of tea and coffee as beverages.

Similarities

- Usually drunk hot.
- Can be drunk without food.
- Can be taken with a snack or meal.
- Can be drunk with milk.
- Can be taken with honey, sugar or sweeteners.
- Both contain caffeine.
- Both can be addictive.

Contrasts

- Differences in taste.
- Tea perhaps preferred at night.
- Differences in caffeine content.

- Coffee more bitter.
- Coffee sometimes taken with cream or whiskey.
- Each perhaps preferred with different foods.
- Coffee preferred for hangover.

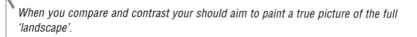

> When you compare and contrast your should aim to paint a true picture of the full 'landscape'.

Whenever evaluation is requested

A worked example of evaluation – TV soap opera director:

Imagine that you are a TV director for a popular soap opera. You have observed in recent months that you have lost some viewers to an alternative soap opera on a rival channel. All is not yet lost because you still have a loyal core of viewers who have remained faithful. Your programme has been broadcast for ten years and there has, until recently, been little change in viewing figures. The rival programme has used some fresh ideas and new actors and has a big novelty appeal. It will take time to see if their level of viewing can be sustained, but you run the risk that you might lose some more viewers at least in the short term. Conversely, with some imagination you might be able to attract some viewers back. However, there have been some recent murmurings about aspects of the programme being stale, repetitive and predictable. You have been given the task of evaluating the programme to see if you can ascertain why you have retained the faithful but lost other viewers, and what you could do to improve the programme without compromising the aspects that work. In your task you might want to review past features (retrospective), outline present features (perspective) and envisage positive future changes (prospective). This illustration may provoke you to think about how you might approach a question that asks you to evaluate some theory or concept in your own academic field of study. Some summary points to guide you are presented below:

- Has the theory/concept stood the test of time?
- Is there a supportive evidence base that would not easily be overturned?
- Are there questionable elements that have been or should be challenged?
- Does more recent evidence point to a need for modification?
- Is the theory/concept robust and likely to be around for the foreseeable future?
- Could it be strengthened through being merged with other theories/concepts?

Write your own checklist on what you remember or understand about each of the following: 'Discuss', 'Compare and Contrast', 'Evaluate' and 'Critique' (just a key word or two for each). If you find this difficult then you should read the section again and then try the exercise.

✓ ....

✓ ....

✓ ....

✓ ....

It should be noted that the words presented in the above examples might not always be the exact words that will appear on your exam script – for example, you might find 'analyse', or 'outline' or 'investigate' and so on. The best advice is to check over your past exam papers and familiarise yourself with the words that are most recurrent.

In summary, this chapter has been designed to give you reference points to measure where you are at in your studies, and to help you map out the way ahead in manageable increments. It should now be clear that learning should not merely be a mechanical exercise, such as just memorising and reproducing study material. Quality learning also involves making connections between ideas, thinking at a deeper level by attempting to understand your material, and developing a critical approach to learning. However, this cannot be achieved without the discipline of preparation for lectures, seminars and exams, or without learning to structure your material (headings and subheadings), and to set each unit of learning within its overall context in your subject and programme. An important device in learning is to develop the ability to ask questions (whether written, spoken or silent). Another useful device in learning is to illustrate your material and use examples that will help make your study fun, memorable and vivid. It is useful to set problems for yourself that will allow you to think through solutions and therefore enhance the quality of your learning.

On the one hand there are the necessary disciplined procedures such as preparation before each learning activity and consolidation afterwards. It is also vital to keep your subject materials in organised folders

so that you can add/extract/replace materials when you need to. On the other hand there is the need to develop personality qualities such as feeding your confidence, fuelling your motivation and turning stress responses to your advantage. This chapter has presented strategies to guide you through finding the balance between these organised and dynamic aspects of academic life.

Your aim should be to become an 'all round student' who engages in and benefits from all the learning activities available to you (lectures, seminars, tutorials, computing, laboratories, discussions, library work, and so on), and to develop all the academic and personal skills that will put you in the driving seat to academic achievement. It will be motivating and confidence building for you, if you can recognise the value of these qualities, both across your academic programme and beyond graduation to the world of work. They will also serve you well in your continued commitment to life-long learning.

References

Adcock, Dennis, Halborg, Al and Ross, Caroline (2001) *Marketing: Principles and Practice*. Harrow: Prentice Hall.

Blythe, Jim (2004) *Essentials of Marketing*. Harlow: Pearson.

Blythe, Jim (2006) *Principles and Practice of Marketing*. London: Thomson Learning.

Brassington, Frances and Pettitt, Stephen, (2002) *Principles of Marketing*. Harlow: Prentice Hall.

Deetz, S.A. (1992) *Democracy in an Age of Corporate Colonization: Developments in Communication and the Politics of Everyday Life*. Albany, NY: State University of New York Press.

Gatignon, Hubert and Robertson, Thomas S. (1985) 'A propositional inventory for new diffusion research', *Journal of Consumer Research*, March: 849–67.

Jobber, David (2003) *Principles and Practice of Marketing*. Maidenhead: McGraw-Hill Education.

Kotler, Philip, Armstrong, Gary, Saunders, John, and Wong, Veronica (2001) *Principles of Marketing (European Edition)*. Harlow: Prentice Hall.

Mantovani, G. (1996) *New Communication Environments: From Everyday to Virtual*. London: Taylor & Francis.

McIlroy, D. (2003) *Studying at University: How to be a Successful Student*. London: SAGE Publications.

Rogers, Everett M. (1962) *Diffusion of Innovation*. New York: Macmillan.

glossary	

Affect	The emotional component of attitude. What one feels about a brand.
Ambient advertising	Commercial messages which become part of the environment.
Aspirational group	A group to which one wishes to belong. The need to belong is likely to lead to purchase of specific items to indicate membership of the group.
Brand	The medium through which marketing activities are focused.
Call to action	The part of the marketing communication which tells the audience what to do next in order to obtain the product.
Classical conditioning	Creating an automatic response in an individual or organism by repetition of a stimulus. This is used in some promotions.
Cognition	The intellectual component of attitude. What one knows about a brand.
Conation	Intended behaviour. What one intends to do about a brand (buy or not buy).
Consideration set	See evoked set.
Consumer	The individual who enjoys the benefits of the product.
Customer	The individual or firm who makes the decision to purchase.

DELPHI	An iterative research technique which elicits a consensus from a group of expert respondents.
Deontology	The philosophical belief that actions can be judged to be ethical or unethical independently of their outcomes.
Differential pricing	See second-market discounting.
Dissociative group	A group to which one does not wish to belong. The desire not to be seen as part of the group is likely to lead to the avoidance of some brands or products.
Economic choice	The decision made between spending money on one item rather than on another.
Evoked set	The group of brands which a consumer chooses between when buying a product.
Focus group	Several individual respondents brought together to discuss a product or brand.
Formal group	A group with a known, recorded membership list, and conditions for entry. These conditions are likely to include product purchases.
Franchise	An agreement for one company to use the brands and business format of another.
Global	Appertaining to the entire world rather than to individual nations.
Grey market	1) Re-import of goods which have been discounted in a second market. 2) Older consumers.
Hedonic	Relating to the pleasurable aspects of ownership.
Hypercompetition	A state of affairs in which competition is so intense companies seek to destabilise the market rather than plan strategically.
Indifference curve	The trade-off in desirability between different quantities of one type of product and different quantities of another.
Informal group	A group with no fixed membership list, and arbitrary rules for entry. Groups of friends are typical of this

group: associating with friends almost always involves shared consumption.

Involvement	Emotional attachment to a brand.
Key account	A strategically-important customer, either for reasons of profit or for reasons of access to other customers and markets.
Logistics	The process of moving raw materials through the value chain to finished products.
Monopolistic competition	A situation where one major company has strong influence on the market, but other firms can still enter.
Monopoly	A situation where one company controls the market.
Need	A felt lack of something.
Normative compliance	The pressure exerted by a group to ensure that norms of behaviour are adhered to. This can include ownership of particular intems or brands.
Odd-even pricing	Ending prices with '99c' or '95p'.
Oligopoly	A situation where a small group of companies control the market between them.
Operant conditioning	Creating an automatic response in an individual or organism with the active co-operation of the subject. This is the basis of most sales promotion and a great deal of advertising.
Perfect competition	A situation where buyers and sellers have perfect knowledge of the market, and where no single buyer or seller can control the market.
Planned obsolescence	The deliberate addition to a product of features which will go out of date or wear out quickly in order to open up the possibility of selling new products.
PLC	Product lifecycle. The stages a product goes through from its introduction to its final withdrawal from the market.
Price elasticity of demand	The extent to which the customer's desire for a product is affected by its price.

Primary group	The people one sees on a daily basis: friends and family.
Primary research	Information collected for the topic currently being investigated.
Publics	Groups or organisations which impact on, or are impacted by, the organisation's activities.
Qualitative data	Research information which cannot be expressed numerically.
Quantitative data	Research information which can be expressed numerically.
Reference group	The people from whom the individual takes behavioural cues.
Secondary group	A group to which one belongs, but which is composed of people who are only infrequently seen. This may include professional associations, which often require specific purchase behaviour.
Secondary research	Research which was collected for a purpose other than the one currently under consideration.
Second-market discounting	Reducing prices charged to one or more segments of the market.
Self-image	The view an individual has of him or herself, moderated by behaviour.
Teleology	The philosophical belief that actions can be judged to be ethical or unethical according to their outcomes: the end justifies the means.
Utilitarian	Relating to the practical aspects of ownership.
Want	A specific satisfier for a need. A brand or product which will fulfil a basic need.

index